GRACE EVANGELICAL SOCIETY

"Faith Alone in Christ Alone"

| VOLUME 34 | Autumn 2021 | NUMBER 67 |

Journal of the
GRACE EVANGELICAL SOCIETY
Published Semiannually by GES

Editor
Kenneth W. Yates

Associate Editors
Robert N. Wilkin
Shawn Lazar

Layout
Shawn Lazar

Manuscripts, book reviews, and other communications should be addressed to GES, Director of Publications, P.O. Box 1308, Denton, TX 76202 or submissions@faithalone.org.

Journal subscriptions, renewals, and changes of address should be sent to the Grace Evangelical Society, P.O. Box 1308, Denton, TX 76202 or email ges@faithalone.org. Subscription Rates: single copy, $9.25 (U.S.); 1 year, $18.50; 2 years, $35.00; 3 years, $49.50; 4 years, $62.00; $13.50 per year for active full-time students. Please add $4.00 for US shipping. Add $4.50 per year for shipping to Mexico and Canada and $8.50 per year for all other international shipping. New subscriptions, 1 year, $9.25; gift subscriptions, 1 year, $9.25.

Purpose: Grace Evangelical Society was formed "to promote the clear proclamation of God's free salvation through faith alone in Christ alone, which is properly correlated with and distinguished from issues related to discipleship."

We Affirm: God, out of love for the human race, sent the Lord Jesus Christ into the world to save sinners. He paid the full penalty for human sin when He died on the cross. Any person who believes in Jesus Christ for everlasting life receives that gift which, as the words *everlasting life* suggest, can never be lost (John 1:29; 3:16-18; 19:30; 1 Tim 1:16).

PRINTED IN THE UNITED STATES OF AMERICA
©2021 Grace Evangelical Society
ISBN: 978-1-943399-43-7

EXAMPLES OF THE FOUR SOILS IN THE GOSPEL OF MARK

KENNETH W. YATES

Editor

I. INTRODUCTION

The Parable of the Four Soils is found in Mark 4:3-8. The Lord interprets the parable in 4:15-20.[1] At face value Jesus says that the Word concerning Him and His coming kingdom will go out through His teaching and the teaching of His disciples. People will respond to that Word in various ways. The Word is like a seed planted in the soil. Each person's response is represented by a particular soil, which pictures how that person's heart receives the Word given to him.

The four soils are the hardened soil on the side of a road, the rocky soil, the thorny soil, and the good soil. Since only the good soil is said to produce an abundant crop—even though there are various degrees of that abundance—many maintain that only this last soil is a picture of believers. Associated with this idea is the belief that all "true" believers will have a good crop of spiritual fruit. The hardened soil, the rocky soil, and the thorny soil all describe different kinds of unbelievers.[2]

However, any fair reading of the parable will not come to those conclusions. There are not three kinds of unbelievers. A hearer either believes or he doesn't. The good soil is not the only one that produces life; the rocky and thorny soils do as well. All three of these soils result in a plant, which is a proof of life. Unbelievers do not have eternal life.

---

[1] Matthew and Luke also contain this parable (Matt 13:3-9; Luke 8:5-8).

[2] John Murray, *Redemption: Accomplished and Applied* (Grand Rapids, MI: Eerdmans, 1955), 153-55; John D. Grassmick, "Mark," *The Bible Knowledge Commentary*, eds. John F. Walvoord and Roy B. Zuck (Wheaton, IL: Victor Books, 1983), 119-20; John F. MacArthur, "The Four Soils: Fertile Ground," https://www.gty.org/library/blog/B170823/the-four-soils-the-fertile-ground. Accessed Jan 4, 2021. Of course, some would modify this view somewhat by saying that the last believers (rocky and thorny) can lose their eternal salvation if they do not produce a crop of good works.

It is not the purpose of this article to address the specifics of the different soils. There are excellent treatments of the subject which the reader can access. This article will start with the assumption that the last three soils describe people who have believed in Jesus Christ for eternal life. In these soils, the issue is not eternal salvation, but fruitfulness. Some believers will not produce a rich spiritual crop in their lives.[3]

After giving the parable, the Lord tells the disciples that it is the key to understanding all of His parables (4:13). It would not be surprising, then, if the reader of Mark's Gospel sees the truths of this parable worked out in the book. In fact, that is exactly what one sees. There are numerous illustrations of the soils, which also serve as warnings and instruction to all the disciples. I will look at these various illustrations, leading up to the Lord's entrance into Jerusalem in chap. 11.

II. THE DISCIPLES IN THE FIRST BOAT SCENE (4:35-41)

In the Gospel of Mark, there are three boat scenes in which the disciples are involved (4:35-41; 6:45-52; 8:13-21). In each instance, the reader sees how these men respond to what the Lord has told them. How do their hearts respond to the seed of Christ's Word? In each case, the disciples come across in a negative light. If we compare them to the different soils, they do not illustrate believers with hearts made up of good soil. While some might conclude they were not believers, this is certainly incorrect. The Gospel of John, particularly, makes it clear they believed (John 1:41-49; 2:11).[4]

This first boat scene occurs immediately after Jesus taught them through parables, including the Parable of the Four Soils (4:33-34). In all of these parables, there is the promise of a coming, eternal kingdom. Jesus is obviously the King of that kingdom. That is the "seed" given to the disciples. Mark wants to make a connection between the

---

[3] Robert N. Wilkin, "How Deep Are Your Spiritual Roots? Luke 8:11-15," *JOTGES* 12 (Spring 1999): 5-12; Zane C. Hodges, *A Free Grace Primer: The Hungry Inherit, The Gospel Under Siege, Grace in Eclipse* (Denton, TX: Grace Evangelical Society, 2011), 51-56; Joseph C. Dillow, *Final Destiny: The Future Reign of the Servant Kings* (Monument, CO: Paniym Group, Inc., 2012), 518-22.

[4] Judas was the lone exception.

teachings of the Lord and this boat scene in v 35. They all happened on the same day.[5]

How did they respond to that teaching? While in the boat with the Lord, a severe storm arises. The disciples are terrified and fear that they are going to die (vv 37-38). They wake up the Lord and plead for Him to save their lives.

The response of the Lord indicates that there was a problem deeper than their fear of dying on the lake. He asks them why they do not have faith (v 40). Since this occurs right after they were taught the parables, the connection strongly suggests that these men did not believe what they had been told in those parables. The faith spoken of here is not the faith that leads to eternal life. This faith involves believing what Jesus just told them in the parables about the coming kingdom. Marshall calls it a faith that involves practical confidence in the power of God to deliver through the miraculous.[6]

The second soil is the rocky soil. The Lord says it represents those who believe the Word spoken, but when hard times come, they fall away. While the falling away in this instance in the boat is not permanent, it is easy to see that the disciples have forgotten what the Lord taught them. They found themselves in difficult circumstances and their faith failed them. When in the boat, they had hearts that could be described as those composed of rocky soil.

III. THE PEOPLE OF GADARA (5:1-20)

After Jesus and the disciples get out of the boat, they come ashore in the land of Gadara.[7] While there, Jesus casts a large number of demons out of a man into a herd of approximately 2,000 pigs. The pigs rush down a cliff and drown in the Sea of Galilee.

Clearly, this man was given a great deliverance by the Lord. His previous condition was well known to the people of the region. They were witnesses of the miraculous power needed to deliver him.

---

[5] France points out this connection. Richard T. France, *The Gospel of Mark: A Commentary on the Greek Text* (Grand Rapids, MI: Eerdmans, 2002), 222.

[6] Christopher D. Marshall, *Faith as a Theme in Mark's Narrative* (Cambridge: Cambridge University Press, 1989), 217-18.

[7] The Critical Text says it is the land of Gerasa.

The Lord spends several hours in the region, and it is certain that He did some teaching. It is clear that He taught the man who previously had the demons about who He is (Mark 5:19-20). Others would have heard this truth as well. How did the people in Gadara respond to the "seed" spread among them in the teaching and power of Christ?

Mark relates how the people became frightened at what they had seen (v 15). They then ask the Lord to depart from that area. At first glance it appears they reject His work and words because they are afraid of the power they have just seen.[8] But more is at play here. The death of 2,000 pigs would have been a tremendous economic loss to the citizens of Gadara. In v 16, the emphasis on the pigs suggests this was the main reason they wanted Him to leave. His actions had cost them a great deal of money.[9]

How should we characterize the spiritual condition of all the people who heard and saw the Lord? No doubt, many did not believe in Him. Their hearts were hardened to the Word of God. Their fear of the supernatural power displayed or the resentment at the loss of their livelihood made them unwilling to consider the possibility that Jesus was the Christ. They were, in the words of the Parable of the Four Soils, like the hardened first soil.

But is it necessary to conclude that this was the case with all those who asked Jesus to leave? Could some have believed in Him as the Christ but still desired that He leave because of the cost His presence might bring? It will be argued later that among the Jews, the preaching of the Word to the masses definitely included believers in the crowd along with the many who did not believe. The man who previously had the demons falls within this category.

If there were believers among the general population of unbelieving Gadara, they are examples of the third, thorny soil. They asked Jesus to leave because they were carried away by the worries of this world and the deceitfulness of riches (4:18-19).

This was not the case with the man who previously had the demons. Even though he had experienced the power of the Lord in a very personal way, he was not afraid. He wanted to follow the Lord in discipleship. In addition, the Lord sent him to proclaim the good

---

[8] H. van der Loos, *The Miracles of Jesus* (Leiden: Brill, 1965), 393.

[9] William L. Lane, *The Gospel According to Mark* (Grand Rapids, MI: Eerdmans, 1974), 187.

news of what Christ had done for him in a region that had rejected the Lord. He faithfully did so. He is a graphic illustration of the fourth soil.

IV. JAIRUS AND THE WOMAN WITH AN ISSUE OF BLOOD (5:21-43)

Jairus is a ruler in the synagogue at Capernaum. The woman with the issue of blood is not named. While one may hold that they are unbelievers, there are arguments for the contrary. We know Jairus' name, which suggests he was known to the early church. In the case of the woman, Jesus tells her that her faith has saved her (v 34). This is the exact same phrase Jesus uses with Bartimaeus in Mark 10:52, and he is certainly seen as a believer. While she was clearly saved from her illness, it is reasonable to conclude that her faith also included believing that Jesus is the Christ and that she was saved spiritually by her faith as well. Williams accurately points out that in Mark's Gospel, these two are minor characters who offer a rebuke and example for the twelve disciples.[10]

These two accounts are an example of intercalation or sandwiching. This means there are two episodes that go together and interpret each other.[11] Both Jairus and the woman are connected by the fact that each grows in his or her faith and overcomes fear and difficulties, and each is associated with the number 12.[12] In addition, in the healing involved with each, Jesus touches a person that would have brought ritual defilement according to official Judaism.

Prior to these two healings, the disciples are fearful and lack faith (4:40-41). In this sense, they were like the people of Gadara (5:15). Jairus is faced with fear as well when he hears that his daughter has died and is told to have faith (v 36). The woman confronts the same issues (vv 33-34). Jairus knows that Jesus can heal his daughter as long as she is alive, but the Lord tells Him to also believe in His ability to raise the dead and to cast his fear aside even though the

---

[10] Joel F. Williams, "Discipleship and Minor Characters in Mark's Gospel," *BibSac* 153 (1996): 338.

[11] James A. Brooks, *Mark* (Nashville, TN: Broadman & Holman, 1991), 73.

[12] Jairus' daughter who died was 12 years old, and the woman had been sick for 12 years.

situation seems hopeless. The woman is called to publicly come forward to proclaim what happened to her.[13] She does this even though she was a social and religious outcast, and her condition was one of private embarrassment.[14]

Both Jairus and the woman overcome their fear. Jairus continues going with the Lord even after his daughter has died and the woman publicly comes forth to explain to the Lord and the crowd what she had done. More importantly, each grew in his or her faith in the sense that each believed new things that the Lord taught him or her. Jairus learned that Jesus could even raise his daughter from the dead. The woman learned that it was not touching the garment of Jesus that saved her from her illness. This is what she thought at first, based upon what she had either seen or heard or even perhaps her superstition (cf. Mark 3:10). Jesus had the authority to heal her by His power, not the magical qualities of His clothes. The connection between Jairus and this woman also involves the fact that this woman was a teaching lesson for him. He saw this woman overcome her fear and take Jesus at His Word. He could do the same.

In other words, both Jairus and the woman grew in their faith. They already believed in Jesus as the Messiah and believed that He could heal. But as they were given new information, they believed what Jesus told them. Throughout Mark, Jesus is teaching the disciples new things. They needed to follow the examples of Jairus and this woman in this regard.

The word about Jesus Christ had reached Jairus and the woman; they had believed it. It would have been easy for Jairus to avoid any association with Jesus. The religious leaders at his synagogue were opposed to Him (3:1-6), and those from Jerusalem had condemned Him (3:22). Whether it was simply the dire circumstances he found himself in with his daughter's illness or the boldness of his faith, he was willing to publicly come to Christ, even if it meant the loss of whatever privileges came his way as a respected leader in the

---

[13] Williams, "Discipleship," 338.

[14] Anybody touching her before she was healed was considered ceremonially unclean and would have to perform a ritual bath (Lev 15:25-27). When she touches the Lord, she does not want anybody to notice her actions. If she was from that particular place and had not traveled a long distance to get there, many in the crowd would have known of her condition. In that case, she would have approached Jesus in as much secrecy as she could have mustered.

synagogue. Neither did he shy away from any persecution that might come his way. His heart was not made up of rocky or thorny soil. While the woman may not have faced the possible persecution Jairus did, she too overcame the difficulties she needed to in order to approach Christ.

Both Jairus and the woman had hearts made up of good soil. They believed what the Lord told them. In them, the reader of Mark learns a lesson about that soil. Discipleship involves growing in faith when it comes to new things. The fourth soil is one that when it hears these new things, it casts aside fear and believes what the Word of God says. The twelve disciples could learn a lesson from these two minor characters.

V. PEOPLE IN JESUS' HOMETOWN (6:1-6)

Mark records a trip that the Lord makes to His hometown of Nazareth. It is a particularly sad event. He speaks in the synagogue and the people know that He has performed many miracles. When He speaks, they also recognize He is a man with profound wisdom.

The "seed" of His Word goes out to them. How do they respond? They were *offended* by Him (v 3). The expression *they were offended* (*eskandalizontō*) carries with it the idea of deep rejection and denial.[15] Since Jesus was a common laborer who grew up in Nazareth and the people of the town knew His family, they concluded that He could not be the Christ. Nobody with such a common background could be the long-awaited promised king.

Lane suggests that the depth of their rejection is seen in their recognition of His power and wisdom. These things had to come from some source. Since they had concluded that Jesus was not sent from God, such supernatural power had to come from Satan. This is what certain religious leaders had concluded as well (3:22). Jesus "marveled" at such unbelief (v 6). This is the only place in the NT where Jesus has this reaction in a negative situation.[16]

The unbelief at Nazareth is a clear example of the hardened first soil in the Parable of the Four Soils. The vast majority of people in

---

[15] *BDAG*, s.v. "*skandalizō*," 926; France, *Mark*, 243

[16] The only other instance when Jesus "marvels" at something is when He marvels at the great faith of the centurion in Matt 8:10.

the town were not willing to listen. Their hearts were hardened to the truth Jesus taught and showed them. The seed of Christ's Word could not penetrate that hardness.

But even in this terribly sad situation, not all is bleak. Even at Nazareth, there appears to be some spiritual success. Mark tells us that Jesus was even able to heal a few people in Nazareth (v 5). There were some there who were open to what He was doing.

It is also completely reasonable to conclude there were even a few who were open to what He was teaching. In fact, Mark relates how He continued teaching in the surrounding area (v 6). In the Parable of the Four Soils, the Lord said that people will respond to His Word in four different ways. What the Lord taught in Nazareth and the surrounding area did not fall only on hardened hearts.

We should not conclude that whenever a crowd of people heard the Lord, all responded in the same way. Dillow points out a common, probably incorrect, practice of Bible readers. Whenever the reader of the NT reads about a crowd or the "multitude," there is a tendency to contrast them with the disciples and conclude that the crowd is made up of unbelievers.[17] There is no reason to see the multitudes in Mark in that way. It also does not make sense logically, since a large group of people will not react in uniformity to what they hear. In the crowds, there were certainly some believers.[18] In at least one instance, Jesus says that the "multitude" was made up of believers (Mark 3:32-34). In Mark 7:14-15 the "crowd" is contrasted to the unbelieving Pharisees. Jesus calls the crowd to Him in order to teach those who are a part of it. The most natural implication is that there were those in the crowd who had believed in Him.

Put simply, Jesus spoke to large crowds. When He did so, the hearts of the different hearers were made up of different kinds of soils. In the rest of Mark 6, there is another example of the Lord speaking to a large group, as well as the account of the disciples doing so.

---

[17] Dillow, *Final Destiny*, 265.

[18] Paul S. Minear, "Audience Criticism and Markan Ecclesiology," in *Neues Testament und Geschichte* (Tübingen: Mohr, 1972), 79-89.

VI. THE MISSION OF THE TWELVE AND THE FEEDING OF THE 5,000 (6:7-13, 30; 31-44)

In Mark 6, Jesus sends out the twelve disciples in order to continue His work in the towns and villages of Galilee. When He called them to be His disciples, He told them they would be fishers of men (1:17). They now begin that process. They proclaim the same message and perform the same miracles that He did (1:15; 6:12-13).

This mission is discussed in all three Synoptic Gospels (Matt 10:1ff; Luke 9:1-6). However, only Mark mentions that when they returned, they told the Lord all that they had *taught* the people (6:30). They were also able to cast out many demons and heal many sick people. Their message certainly included the fact that Jesus was the Christ. They were now spreading the seed of God's Word. The miracles they performed through the authority Christ gave them demonstrated the veracity of their message.

According to the Jewish historian Josephus, Galilee at the time of Christ had over 200 villages and was heavily populated.[19] With all twelve disciples going out teaching, a large group of people would have heard the message. The seed would have been sown in many hearts, and there would have been many different kinds of responses. While some did not believe, others did. Among those who believed, there would have been different levels of commitment to following the Lord. At least some of those who had believed wanted to know more and sought to do so.

In Mark's account, immediately after the disciples returned from their mission, Jesus wanted to take them to a lonely place for rest (6:30-31). However, this was not possible because there was a large crowd of people coming to them. No doubt, this crowd was due in large part to the successful teaching tour of the disciples. They had come to hear more not only from the disciples, but also from the One about whom the disciples had preached. They were following the disciples for that very purpose. In other words, they were seeking to hear and be with the Lord.

Jesus spends many hours teaching them in this deserted place. While, once again, some might say this crowd was made up entirely

---

[19] Flavius Josephus, *The Works of Josephus*, trans. William Whiston (Carol Stream, IL: Tyndale House, 1980), *Vita* 45; *Bellum Judaicum* 3.3.2.

of unbelievers, this would be highly unlikely. There are no reported miracles performed by the Lord during those hours of teaching.[20] The people stayed during these long hours without food or water. This demonstrated their commitment to Him at least at some level. Because of the Lord's compassion on them, He miraculously feeds them in the wilderness with only a few fish and loaves of bread. This display of power would have helped demonstrate the truth of what He had taught them for all those hours.

It strains belief to conclude that the Lord did not speak of Himself and the coming kingdom of God. This is what Jesus proclaimed (1:15).[21] In fact, in John's account, many in the crowd followed the Lord the next day, and He told them of their need to believe in Him for eternal life (John 6:22-40).

Mark tells us that Jesus fed a multitude which consisted of 5,000 men. Since this number did not include women or children (Matt 14:21), the total number who heard the words of Jesus that day probably numbered over 10,000.[22] Jesus sees Himself as the shepherd of this large group (Mark 6:34). That is why He feeds them both physically with bread and spiritually with His Word. Their religious and political leaders had abandoned them.[23] Of the more than 10,000 individuals present, most would have been unbelievers. These would have been people who perhaps were there simply to see some miracle performed. But there also would have been believers of various stripes in the group. Some would have feared being publicly associated with Christ and the consequences of such an association (rocky soil). Some would have not wanted to follow the Lord because they loved the

---

[20] Matthew does mention that the Lord healed their sick prior to teaching, but Mark does not (Matt 14:14).

[21] Jesus preached a message of repentance, as did John the Baptist. This is *not* the same message believers today proclaim, at least not to unbelievers. Repentance, when defined as turning from sin, is not a requirement of receiving eternal life. Jesus and John preached to the nation of Israel. For the kingdom to come to the nation, the nation *as a whole* was required to turn from their sin. The point of this article is that when the disciple of the Lord proclaims God's word, in whatever age and to whatever audience, people will respond differently. For a discussion on the meaning of repentance and how it is not a part of receiving eternal life, see Zane C. Hodges, *Absolutely Free,* Second Edition (Corinth, TX: Grace Evangelical Society, 2014), 146-50. All of chapter 12 deals with repentance.

[22] John A. Martin, "Luke," *The Bible Knowledge Commentary,* eds. John F. Walvoord and Roy B. Zuck (Wheaton, IL: Victor Books, 1983), 229.

[23] In the previous chapter, Mark records the evil character of the political "shepherd" of the people, Herod Antipas (Mark 6:14-29).

comfort of their lives (thorny soil). But some, after seeing His power and hearing His Word would have desired to follow Him and learn more from Him.

Even though Wiersbe sees this crowd in a mostly negative light, he recognizes that there were believers in it. He says that the crowd failed to understand the "spiritual message" of Christ's teaching and followed Him only for the help He gave them when He fed them. However, he acknowledges that this was only for the "most part."[24] There were some who followed Christ with good and noble hearts. This agrees with the proposition that there were other types of soil among the crowd, other than the hardened soil. This writer would add that we simply cannot determine the percentage of each type of soil in such a large crowd.

Later, Jesus leaves the predominately Jewish Galilee and travels to a mostly Gentile area. Mark records two instances where multitudes are exposed to the Lord. In one case, in Decapolis,[25] He heals a deaf man who also had difficulty speaking. It is clear that He did other things because the multitude concludes that He had done *all* things well, even healing the deaf and dumb (7:31-37). This certainly indicates that the hearts of many people in that region were open to what He was doing and saying. There would have been different responses to the seed Christ was sowing in Decapolis.

This is supported by the fact that immediately after the reaction of the people in Decapolis, Mark records another account of Jesus feeding a multitude. He connects this with the people in Decapolis by saying that this feeding took place "in those days" (8:1). Once again, it is a desert area (8:4), and in this case the people remain with the Lord for three days. Many of them had also traveled at a great distance to be with Him (8:3). The cost of being with Him was that they were experiencing hunger because of lack of food.

This crowd numbered in the thousands (8:9). Matthew states that Jesus healed many sick people (Matt 15:31), but in three days the Lord would have also taught the people many things. There would have been many there who did not need healing. Among this group

---

[24] Warren W. Wiersbe, *The Bible Exposition Commentary* (Wheaton, IL: Victor Books, 1996), 1:132.

[25] The word *Decapolis* literally means *ten cities*. Nine of the ten cities were east of the Jordan River in Gentile territory. See, Barry K. Mershon, Jr., "Mark," *The Grace New Testament Commentary*, ed. Robert N. Wilkin (Denton, TX: Grace Evangelical Society, 2019), 90.

would have been believers in what Jesus was teaching. These believers would have been made up of the last three soils in the Parable of the Four Soils. The positive descriptions Mark gives of these individuals demand such a conclusion.

Whenever the Lord spoke to these large crowds, especially when He did so over a long period of time, the words of the Lord Himself suggests that there would have been all four types of soils among the people. When Jesus gave the parable, He said that when the sower spread the seed of His Word, that seed would come to rest on all four (Mark 4:3-8). Among thousands of listeners, this would certainly be the case.

VII. DISCIPLES AND THE SECOND AND THIRD BOAT SCENES (6:45-52; 8:12-21)

The second boat scene involving the disciples occurs after the feeding of the 5,000. The Lord comes to them, walking on the water in the midst of a strong wind storm. They think Jesus is a ghost and are frightened (6:50). This is the same reaction they had in the first boat scene.

When the Lord gets into the boat with them, the wind stopped and they are amazed. Mark says that the reaction of the disciples was because they had not understood what happened when Jesus fed the 5,000. In that feeding, Jesus showed that He would meet the needs of His sheep. He was their Shepherd, just as God was the Shepherd of His people in Psalm 23. As a result, they had nothing to fear.

In this example, the disciples did not believe what Jesus had revealed to them. Their hearts were not receptive to this new information. It is of interest that Mark says that their hearts were "hardened" (6:52). This description reminds the reader of the first soil, where the seed of God's Word cannot penetrate the ground it falls on. In fact, in Mark 3:5 the unbelieving Pharisees are described as having hard hearts. The disciples were believers, but their hearts were too hard to understand the new truth Jesus had just taught them.

In the third boat scene, a similar thing occurs. After seeing Jesus miraculously feed the 4,000, the disciples think that the Lord is not pleased with them because they did not bring bread with them. Once again, He rebukes them for not learning from what He has taught them. How could they possibly conclude that He was concerned about the amount of bread they had brought, after they had seen Him feed thousands of people with a few loaves of bread? As in the second boat scene, He points out that their hearts are hardened.

But He adds a further rebuke. He quotes from the OT and asks if they were blind and lacked understanding (8:18). Earlier, He had used such imagery to describe unbelievers who were on the "outside" (4:12). Those on the outside did not understand the things Jesus taught.

The reference to the hardness of hearts of the believing disciples in Mark is telling. This, along with their blindness and inability to understand what Jesus was saying, indicates that they were acting like unbelievers. We must conclude that when it comes to appropriating spiritual truths, believers can indeed act in that way. When that happens, the heart of the believer is like the first soil. Hornok suggests that these words by the Lord were an attack on the pride of the disciples. Perhaps they thought they had hearts represented by the good soil because of their closeness to the Lord and that He had privately explained the meaning of the parable to them (4:10-20). In practice, however, they were acting like those outside of this favored position.[26] This would have been a call for them to take heed to how they responded to all the things Christ was teaching them.

As the Book of Mark progresses, the Twelve continue to struggle with understanding the Lord's instruction. As He teaches them about the suffering that will result from following Him, they are not able to understand. James and John demonstrate a heart made up of thorny soil as they reveal that they are more interested in power, prestige, and getting ahead of others than suffering for Christ (Mark 10:35-37).

VIII. BARTIMAEUS: A GREAT EXAMPLE OF THE FOURTH SOIL (10:46-52)

Blind Bartimaeus is an important person in Mark's Gospel. He is the only person Jesus heals who is named in the book. He is the only one in the book who calls Jesus the Son of David, a Messianic title. He is one who gains his sight, which is a picture of spiritual insight as

---

[26] Marcia Hornok, "Excavating the Parable of the Sower: Discerning Jesus' Meaning," *Journal of Dispensational Theology* 19 (2015): 195.

well. When the reader considers this man, there can be no doubt that he was a believer. But he was more than that. He becomes a model for others to follow.[27] He is an example of the fourth soil.

Bartimaeus has heard about the deeds and words of Jesus. He knew that Jesus had healed others just like him. He knew that the Messiah would be able to heal. All of his actions show that his heart is fertile ground for the things he has heard. That heart is not rocky. He does not let difficulties prevent him from coming to Jesus and following Him. He is blind and an outcast in that society. As a result, the people tell him to be quiet when he calls out to the Lord. It would have been easy to conclude that Jesus could not be bothered by someone as insignificant as he was. Yet, he continues to call out to the Lord. When he is healed, he follows Him on the difficult road to Jerusalem, where Jesus will meet His ignoble death.

But his heart is not thorny either. His meager possessions, whatever they might be, are nothing compared to being with the Lord. He tosses aside his important coat and whatever alms were in it when the Lord calls him.

In following Jesus on the road to Jerusalem, Bartimaeus is following in His path of suffering. No doubt, the Lord taught him more as they traveled that road together. Bartimaeus is presented in such a positive light that the reader is left with the impression that his heart will believe and that he will act upon the things he learns as he leaves Jericho with the Lord. He becomes an outstanding example of a believer whose heart firmly grasps the words of the Lord and bears much fruit.

IX. CONCLUSION

The Parable of the Four Soils in Mark 4 is a key part of Christ's teaching. He Himself says it is a basic part of what He teaches the disciples. If they don't understand it, they won't be able to understand the other parables He gives them. Not surprisingly, the application of this parable can be seen throughout the book.

It is unfortunate that many have grossly misunderstood such an important parable. They begin with their theological view that all true Christians are fruit bearing, and therefore the thorny and rocky soils must represent unbelievers. This not only contradicts Christian experience, but Mark shows that believers can indeed respond in ways that do not produce spiritual fruit. This is most clearly seen in the twelve disciples who were closest to the Lord. Of all the Synoptic Gospels, Mark paints a picture of the disciples which indicates that even though they were believers and had eternal life, they did not have hearts made up of good soil when it came to taking in the teachings of the Lord.

When the Lord spoke in parables, He indicated that it was of extreme importance that the person listening to Him should be careful how He listens (Mark 4:9, 23-24). Marshall is correct when he says that this is especially true with the Parable of the Four Soils. He states that, "the parable is concerned with the way in which men hear the Word of God, and constitutes a summons to them to take care how they hear it."[28]

Interpreters can quibble over the parable's main audience. Hornok maintains that the first soil can be applied to unbelievers but holds that the *main* idea of the parable is not about the eternal salvation of those who hear the Word of God. Jesus is talking to the disciples and tells them to be careful how they hear. The hardness of their hearts in the boat scenes shows that believers can be represented in the first soil. Her view is that the primary purpose of all four soils is to be an admonition to believers. The Word of God needs to grow, bear fruit, and reproduce itself. In order for that to happen, it needs to find a fertile heart in the believer. If believers do not listen carefully with a receptive heart, the Word can be stolen, starved or strangled.[29] Once again, the example of the disciples in Mark provides a lesson of how believers can refuse to believe new truth from God's Word.

However, it can also be maintained that the *primary* reference of the first soil is to unbelievers.[30] Those who hear the Word and are not willing to believe, for whatever reason, do not have life. But it is also

---

[28] I. Howard Marshall, *The Gospel of Luke* (Grand Rapids, MI: Eerdmans, 1978), 318.

[29] Hornok, "Excavating," 198.

[30] In the Lukan version of the parable, a comparison of Luke 8:12 and 8:13 shows that the first soil there unambiguously represents unbelievers only. However, the Lord taught His parables on many different occasions and in different ways. It is possible, therefore, that when the Lord presented the parable as recorded in Mark that He did not intend the first soil to be understood as exclusively representing unbelievers.

clear, based upon the example of the disciples, that believers can act like unbelievers when they do not grow in their knowledge of God's Word and put it into practice.

Regardless of the main emphasis, Mark makes it clear that believers can learn from observing all four soils and how they each respond to God's Word. Believers should constantly ask themselves: What is the condition of my heart? Do I believe what God reveals to me in His Word?

But believers can also learn another example from the disciples. The condition of our heart is not a static thing. It can change. If, like the disciples, I find that I am receiving the Word of God with a rocky or thorny heart, I do not have to leave it in that condition. Even though Mark paints the bleakest picture of the disciples, all students of the Bible know that the instruction of the Lord produced great results in these men. It is not a guarantee, but the Lord can do the same thing in any believer's life. We can be like Bartimaeus!

This parable also leaves us with a strong encouragement. Like the Lord and the disciples, we too can sow the seed of God's Word. If we are faithful in doing so, we can expect that there will be some who respond positively. Some will not believe. But some will. And among those who do, some will even produce much fruit.

DIFFERENT MEANINGS OF SALVATION IN FIVE NEW TESTAMENT BOOKS

ROBERT N. WILKIN

Associate Editor

I. INTRODUCTION

Tremendous confusion results when one misinterprets the meaning of *sōzō* and *sōtēria*. It is not simply laypeople who wrongly assume that the words *saved* and *salvation* in the NT almost always refer to regeneration. Many scholars do as well. But there is good reason to believe that these words often refer to something other than regeneration and that in specific books the sense is both different and consistent. Knowing that opens up the understanding of these books.

Recently I wrote an article on three specific uses of *sōzō* in 1 Corinthians. I showed that it is highly likely that in those three uses (1 Cor 3:15; 5:5; 15:2), the salvation in view is being spiritually healthy, not being saved from eternal condemnation. In this article I will consider the uses of *sōzō* ("save") and *sōtēria* ("salvation") in five NT books. It is my contention that in each of these books, the meaning of those words is consistent and does not refer to salvation from eternal condemnation there.

II. THE RANGE OF MEANING FOR SOTĒRIA AND *SŌZŌ* IN THE NT

The words *sōtēria* and *sōzō* have a range of meanings in the NT, including:

- Regeneration/salvation from eternal condemnation (e.g., John 3:16-17; Eph 2:5, 8; Titus 3:5)
- Deliverance from impending death (Matt 8:25)
- Healing from illness (Jas 5:15)
- Being spiritually well (1 Cor 3:15; 5:5; 15:2)

- Handling trials in a God-honoring fashion (Phil 1:19; 2:12)
- Being chosen to be one of Christ's partners in the life to come (Heb 1:14; 5:9)
- Deliverance from false teachers and their practices (1 Tim 4:16)
- Experiencing joy and contentment in the face of trying circumstances (1 Tim 2:15)
- Deliverance from temporal judgment from God/the death dealing consequences of sin (Jas 1:21; 2:14; 5:20)
- Deliverance from the coming Tribulation (1–2 Thessalonians).

III. THREE USES OF *SŌTĒRIA* IN PHILIPPIANS: HANDLING PERSECUTION IN A GOD-HONORING WAY

Two of the three uses of *sōtēria* in Philippians are recognized by all scholars as not referring to salvation from eternal condemnation. Those verses are Phil 1:19 and Phil 1:28.

Philippians 1:19. Paul was in prison in Rome as he wrote this epistle, one of the four Prison Epistles. He wrote,

> For I know that this will turn out for my deliverance [*sōtēria*] through your prayers and the supply of the Spirit of Jesus Christ, according to my earnest expectation and hope that in nothing I shall be ashamed, but with all boldness, as always, so now also Christ will be magnified in my body, whether by life or by death. For to me, to live is Christ, and to die is gain. But if I live on in the flesh, this will mean fruit from my labor; yet what I shall choose I cannot tell (Phil 1:19-22).

Paul already knew he had everlasting life and was secure (Eph 2:8-9; 2 Tim 1:12). But the salvation he speaks of in Phil 1:19 is related to his imprisonment as the following verses show. But in what sense did he know that he would gain his salvation through the prayers of the Philippians and the work of the Spirit in his life?

Robert Lightner says that the salvation here is not being born again, but that it refers "to either the final stage of his salvation (cf. Rom. 5:9) or future vindication in a Roman court."[1]

---

[1] Robert P. Lightner, "Philippians" in *The Bible Knowledge Commentary*, eds. John F. Walvoord and Roy B. Zuck (Wheaton, IL: Victor Books, 1985), 2:651.

Fee understands this salvation as being "vindicated," that is, "that Christ be 'magnified'"[2] through Paul's imprisonment.

O'Brien also sees the issue here as vindication. He points out that Paul is here quoting Job 13:16. Just as Job was ultimately vindicated by handling his suffering well, Paul is confident that he too will be vindicated by handling his suffering well.[3]

In sum, most commentators understand *sōtēria* here to refer to vindication before the Lord for having handled his suffering well.

Verses 20-22 explain that the salvation Paul has in mind is handling his persecution "with all boldness" with the result that "Christ will be magnified in my body, whether by life or by death." He was not saying that he was sure that he would be released from prison, since he indicates that "what I shall choose I cannot tell."

Philippians 1:28. Paul's second reference to *sōtēria* deals with the readers:

> Only let your conduct be worthy of the gospel of Christ, so that whether I come and see you or am absent, I may hear of your affairs, that you stand fast in one spirit, with one mind striving together for the faith of the gospel, and not in any way terrified by your adversaries, which is to them a proof of perdition, but to you of salvation [*sōtēria*], and that from God. For to you it has been granted on behalf of Christ, not only to believe in Him, but also to suffer for His sake, having the same conflict which you saw in me and now hear is in me (Phil 1:27-30).

Paul links their salvation with his. They are to follow his example by handling their trials so that they too continue boldly "to suffer for His sake." They were to maintain "the same conflict which you saw in me and now hear is in me."

Fee comments on the connection between 1:19 and 1:28 and says that "the word 'salvation' probably carries a sense very close to that in v. 19. Such salvation/vindication will not necessarily be manifest to the opponents, but it will become clear to the believers themselves."[4]

---

[2] Gordon D. Fee, *Paul's Letter to the Philippians* (Grand Rapids, MI: Eerdmans, 1995), 126.

[3] Peter T. O'Brien, *The Epistle to the Philippians* (Grand Rapids, MI: Eerdmans, 1991), 108.

[4] Fee, *Philippians*, 169-70.

Some commentators, however, do not mention the connection between Phil 1:19 and 1:28. Lightner fails to point that out, and he is not quite clear how he understands 1:28 when he writes, "Instead they were to be reminded at such times that their own victorious Christian response would be a sign that their opposers would eventually be destroyed. At the same time, it would be a sign that the saints of God would be delivered by God Himself."[5]

O'Brien also fails to mention the connection. He understands the salvation here as entering into Christ's eschatological kingdom.[6]

In Phil 1:19 and 1:28, *sōtēria* refers to a believer who handles his ongoing persecution in a way that brings glory and honor to our Lord. The believer who does so will be vindicated at the Judgment Seat of Christ.

The third use, Phil 2:12, is understood by many commentators to refer to gaining or maintaining everlasting life by doing good works. Lightner says, for example:

> It is commonly understood that this exhortation relates to the personal salvation of the saints at Philippi. They were told to "work out," to put into practice in their daily living, what God had worked in them by His Spirit. They were not told to work for their salvation but to work out the salvation God had already given them.[7]

Similarly, though Fee does see a connection with 1:28, he writes,

> This is not a soteriological text per se, dealing with "people getting saved" or "saved people persevering." Rather it is an ethical text, dealing with "how saved people live out their salvation" in the context of the believing community and the world. What Paul is referring to, therefore, is the present "outworking" of their eschatological salvation within the believing community in Philippi.[8]

O'Brien takes a view that is close to that of Fee, a view that has been held by many commentators over the past hundred years:

> *Sōtēria* is being used in a sociological rather than a strictly theological sense to describe the spiritual health

[5] Lightner, "Philippians," 652.
[6] O'Brien, *Philippians*, 156.
[7] Lightner, "Philippians," 655.
[8] Fee, *Philippians*, 235.

and well-being of the entire community at Philippi. Paul is therefore urging all the Christians corporately to take whatever steps are necessary to remove every trace of spiritual disease and thus to restore the congregation to health and wholeness.[9]

If we pay attention to the context of the third use, we will see that it too refers to vindication before Christ that will result from persevering in the handling of persecution in a God-honoring manner.

Philippians 2:12. The first thing that should be noticed is that this is the third and final reference to *sōtēria* in Philippians. Then one should notice the comparison between "my *sōtēria*" in 1:19 and "your own *sōtēria*" in 2:12. Whatever Paul means by "my *sōtēria*" clearly informs us what he means by "your own *sōtēria*." Finally, the ensuing context after Phil 2:12 shows that the theme of handling persecution in a God-honoring fashion fits perfectly in this third use.

Paul says, "Therefore, my beloved, as you have always obeyed, not as in my presence only, but now much more in my absence, work out your own salvation [*sōtēria*] with fear and trembling" (Phil 2:12). To "work out your own salvation with fear and trembling" is to continue to obey ("as you have always obeyed...work out your *sōtēria*"). In light of 1:28 and 2:14-16, what Paul is commanding is that they are to continue to "shine as lights in the world" (v 15) by "holding fast the word of life" (v 16) so that at the Judgment Seat of Christ ("the day of Christ"), Paul might be able to rejoice since their fruitfulness will show that his labors among them were not in vain.

All three uses of *sōtēria* in Philippians refer to persevering by handling one's persecution for Christ in a manner that glorifies Him. If we wish to retain the idea of *deliverance*, then we could say that *sōtēria* in Philippians is being delivered from shame both now and at the Judgment Seat of Christ. That deliverance is achieved by keeping a proper perspective on suffering for Christ that results in persevering in one's trials in a way that glorifies God.

Even if the NT taught that salvation *from eternal condemnation* was conditioned upon perseverance in good works, Phil 1:19, 1:28, and 2:12 can easily be seen as not referring to salvation from eternal condemnation. One would need to go elsewhere to find that teaching;

---

[9] O'Brien, *Philippians*, 277.

but, of course, it is not found anywhere since the sole condition of salvation from eternal condemnation is faith in Christ.

IV. FIVES USES OF *SŌZŌ* IN JAMES: ESCAPING TEMPORAL JUDGMENT VIA PUTTING OUR FAITH TO WORK

All commentators understand Jas 5:15 as referring to healing or deliverance from an illness. Most commentators suggest that Jas 4:12 refers to God's ability to extend or curtail one's physical life.

Three of the uses of *sōzō* in James are widely understood by commentators to refer to deliverance from eternal condemnation (Jas 1:21; 2:14; 5:20). However, there is strong contextual support for the view that even those three uses also refer to deliverance from temporal judgment.

James 1:21. The author has just called the readers "my beloved brethren" (1:16, 19). In fact, in the verse before 1:19-21, James says "He brought us forth by the word of truth" (1:18). To be *brought forth* (*apekuēsin, He birthed us*) is to be born again, to be given everlasting life. There is no shift in addressees in vv 19-21. James is challenging his born-again readers to receive the Word of God that had been implanted in them through the preaching of God's Word. Application of God's Word is necessary "to save your souls," that is, *to save your lives* from the death dealing consequences of sin (Jas 1:15).

That understanding, however, is not reflected in most commentaries. Adamson is representative of the view of many:

> The reference to salvation is to be interpreted in the light of the rapidly approaching Day of Judgment (see Acts 17:30). It is charged with the eschatological urgency of the NT, including (conspicuously) the Epistle of James. No soul can be called saved, or lost, until the Final Judgment; hence James's gospel of faith continuing at work in hope of that final approbation, 1:3. It is faith expressed in action (*magna efficacia*, Bengel) that puts the power of the divine Word into human life, to the saving of the soul at the Last Judgment.[10]

---

[10] James B. Adamson, *The Epistle of James* (Grand Rapids, MI: Eerdmans, 1976), 81–82.

James 2:14. Much confusion has been caused by this simple verse. James is obviously saying that faith without works cannot save the believer. But the issue, often not considered, is what the believer needs to be saved *from.* The believer already has passed from death into life (John 5:24), is already guaranteed that he will never perish (John 3:16; 11:26), and has already been saved (Eph 2:8). What the believer needs salvation from are the consequences that result from failing to apply God's Word. "What does it profit, my brethren, if someone says he has faith but does not have works? Can faith save him?"

The issue is stated in the opening words, "What does it profit (*ti to ophelos*)?" A believer will only be *profited* if he not only *says* the right things, but also *does* the right things. James had just said, "So speak and so do as those who will be judged by the law of liberty" (Jas 2:12).

The believer ("my brethren") who "says he has faith" but who does not do what is consistent with what he believes ("but does not have works") is one who will not be saved from God's temporal judgment.

Like a good preacher, James illustrates his point. If a brother or sister in your own assembly is hungry and poorly clothed, it is not enough to *say,* "Be warmed and filled" (v 16). Instead, you must also *do,* that is, you must "give them the things which are needed for the body." A failure to do so "does not profit" the believer in need (v 16). Notice that v 16 ends with the same question that began v 14 (*ti to ophelos*).

Faith without works will not save from God's temporal judgment. It is dead, that is, it is unprofitable. Like a dead battery in a car, when we do not have faith to do what we believe, our faith is unprofitable for us or the believers who need our help.

Unfortunately, many commentators fail to consider the context sufficiently. Peter Davids's interpretation is representative of the view of most commentators:

> That which will be useless in the final judgment is a faith lacking works. The hypothetical situation introduced by *ean* is described as a person "claiming to have faith." And a claim it is, for whatever the content of the faith in terms of orthodox belief, pious expressions, prayers, etc., it appears only in the person's verbalizations (and ritual actions) but not in such deeds as would prove the reality of

an eschatological hope…Works are not an "added extra" to faith, but are an essential expression of it.[11]

James 5:19-20. Some Roman Catholic expositors understand these verses to mean that if a believer turns a straying believer back to the Lord, he covers a multitude of *his own sins* (i.e., the sins of the rescuer, not the one he rescues) and makes *his own salvation* more likely. As Catholic apologist John Martignoni writes,

> Did you catch that? Most people who read this passage do not stop to think about what it is really saying. If you do something to bring a sinner back from the error of his way, you will save YOUR soul from death and will cover a multitude of YOUR sins. What an awesome promise God has given us in Scripture! Zeal for the souls of others will cover a multitude of our sins and save our soul from death![12]

Protestant commentator Adamson takes the salvation as that of the one who strayed, but concerning the covering of sins he writes, "These sins are obviously the sins of the reclaimer, not the reclaimed."[13]

Protestant expositors are divided as to what type of salvation is in view. Some understand James to be speaking of salvation from eternal condemnation and some from physical death. Adamson understands this salvation as both from physical death and eternal condemnation: "The soul is that of the erring brother; see 1:21. Death, from which he is saved, is the penalty of sin, as in 1:15, and under the covenant 'final exclusion from the Divine Society' (1 John 5:16; so Westcott)."[14]

Davids agrees that both types of death are in view:

> The concept of saving a soul from death is clear enough, for death is plainly the final result of sin, usually thought of as eternal death or the last judgment (Dt. 30:19; Jb. 8:13; Pss. 1:6; 2:12; Pr. 2:18; 12:28; 14:12; Je. 23:12; Jude 1:23…). That sin can result in physical death is also clear (1 Cor. 15:30 [sic][15], as well as many of the above OT examples) and this may be part of James's meaning (as in

---

[11] Peter H. Davids, *The Epistle of James* (Grand Rapids, MI: Eerdmans, 1982), 120–21.

[12] At https://www.biblechristiansociety.com/newsletter/389-planting-seeds-of-faith-with-your-help.

[13] Adamson, *James*, 204.

[14] Ibid., 203.

[15] He meant 1 Cor 11:30.

5:14-16), but the tone appears to go beyond physical death and recognizes death as an eschatological entity, at least where one dies in sin (cf. 1:15).[16]

Other Protestant commentators interpret Jas 5:20 to refer exclusively (or primarily) to eternal condemnation. Moo, for example, writes, "It is by sharing with James the conviction that there is indeed an eternal death, to which the way of sin leads, that we shall be motivated to deal with sin in our lives and in the lives of others."[17] Stulac agrees: "But when he speaks of saving the sinner's *psychēn*, 'soul,' from death, he 'appears to go beyond physical death and recognize death as an eschatological entity' (Davids 1982: 200)."[18]

Still other Protestant commentators understand James to be speaking only of salvation from physical death. For example, Johnson gives no indication that he understands death here to include eternal condemnation:

> The connection of sin and death is widespread (see Deut 30:19; Job 8:13; Pss 1:6; 2:12; Prov 2:18; 12:28; 14:12; Wis 2:24; Rom 5:12; 1 Cor 15:56; 2 Bar. 85:13; T. Abr. 10:2–15). The "rescue operation" by moral correction vividly recalls the imagery of 1:15, which describes the inexorable progress from desire to sin and from sin to death (*thanatos*). In Matt 18:15, the result of such correction is "gaining your brother" (*ekerdēsas ton adelphon sou*). Ezekiel also spoke of the prophetic rebuke in terms of life and death: "If you warn the righteous man not to sin and he does not sin, he surely shall live, because he took warning; and you will have saved your life" (Ezek 3:21).[19]

Richardson too speaks of physical death as the issue here: "James's focus is on the death of the body. He was not commenting on that which will follow the judgment of God (cf. 4:12), who will cause the destruction of the wicked."[20]

Hodges says that the rescuer is "turning him [the wanderer] aside from a sinful path that can lead him to his physical death (see 1:15).

---

[16] Davids, *James*, 199-200.

[17] Douglas J. Moo, *The Letter of James* (Grand Rapids, MI: Eerdmans, 2000), 251.

[18] George M. Stulac, *James* (Downers Grove, IL: IVP Academic, 1993), 188.

[19] Luke Timothy Johnson, *The Letter of James* (New Haven, CT: Yale University Press, 2008), 338.

[20] Kurt A. Richardson, *James* (Nashville, TN: Broadman & Holman, 1997), 245.

Thus, a Christian's efforts for the restoration of his brother to the pathway of obedience are life-saving in scope."[21]

That believers are the rescuers is clear because the first word in v 19 in both English and Greek is *brethren* (*adelphoi*). Brethren are believers all through James.

That the ones being rescued are believers is also clear because James says, "if *anyone among you* wanders from the truth" (emphasis added). The wanderer is one of the brethren.

That a believer who strays could be called "a sinner" (v 20) is not surprising. In the first place, even believers who are walking in fellowship with God are called sinners in Scripture (e.g., Rom 5:19; Gal 2:17; 1 Tim 1:15). In the second place, an extremely common NT use of *sinners* (*hamartōloi*) refers to those who have strayed and are spiritually away from God (e.g., Matt 9:11; Luke 15:7, 10; John 9:16, 24, 31; 1 Pet 4:18).

When James says that the rescuer "will save a soul [or, life] from death" (v 20), he is referring to saving a fellow believer from imminent physical death. The salvation of the soul (*psychē*) in James (cf. 1:21) and in the rest of the Bible refers to salvation from physical death. Peter, speaking of Noah's ark, says, "eight souls were saved through water" (1 Pet 3:20). Solomon said that God "will spare the poor and needy and will *save the souls* of the needy" (Ps 72:13). He made it clear that he was speaking of physical deliverance when he added, "He will redeem their life from oppression and violence; and precious shall be their blood in His sight" (Ps 72:14). The Apostle John said that Jesus "laid down His life [*psychēn*] for us" (1 John 3:16). Then John went on to say that we should "lay down our lives [*psychas*] for the brethren" (1 John 3:16). The Lord on several occasions spoke of the need of believers to save their lives/souls (Matt 16:25-26; Mark 8:35-36; Luke 9:24-25; 17:33), which has been called "the Lord's logion of the salvation of the *psychē*."[22]

All uses of *sōzō* in James refer to deliverance from temporal judgment.

---

[21] Zane C. Hodges, "The Epistle of James," *The Grace New Testament Commentary,* First Edition, ed. by Robert N. Wilkin (Denton, TX: Grace Evangelical Society, 2010), 1142.

[22] See, Jerry Pattillo, "An Exegetical Study of the Lord's Logion on the 'Salvation of the Psychē,'" *JOTGES* (Autumn 2015):21-36. Available online at https://faithalone.org/wp-content/uploads/2016/12/Autumn_JOTGES2015.pdf.

V. FIVE USES OF *SŌTĒRIA* IN ROMANS: DELIVERANCE FROM TEMPORAL WRATH BY WALKING ACCORDING TO THE SPIRIT

There are thirteen uses of the words *sōtēria* and *sōzō* in Romans. That is too many passages to cover in a journal article, so I have chosen to focus on the five uses of *sōtēria*.

It is not uncommon for commentators to interpret *sōtēria* in Romans as always referring to deliverance from eternal condemnation, though some understand Rom 13:11 as referring to the Rapture. However, there is reason to believe that at least three of the five, and possibly all five, refer to deliverance from God's wrath in this life.

Romans 1:16. Paul says that the gospel of Christ "is the power of God to salvation [*sōtēria*] for everyone who believes." Most commentators understand Paul to be saying that the message of 1 Cor 15:3-11 results in everlasting life for everyone who believes it.[23] Witmer writes, for example, "At least Paul gladly proclaimed it [the gospel] as God's panacea for mankind's spiritual need. He identified it as the infinite resources (*dynamis*, 'spiritual ability') of God applied toward the goal of salvation in the life of everyone who believes regardless of racial background."[24]

The word *gospel* is not defined in its ten uses in Romans.[25] It is reasonable to understand that expression as referring to the good news of the substitutionary death and resurrection of the Lord Jesus Christ (cf. 1 Cor 15:3-11). However, never in Romans, Paul's other epistles, or anywhere in the NT are we told that anyone who believes the gospel is born again. In 1 Cor 15:1-11, the gospel is the message which, *if held firmly to*, results in *ongoing salvation*, that is, ongoing spiritual health (1 Cor 15:2).

In Rom 1:15 Paul said that he was "ready to preach the gospel to you who are in Rome also." Since the readers were already born again (Rom 1:6, 8, 12), Paul's reason for wanting to preach the gospel

---

[23] So, Douglas J. Moo, *The Epistle to the Romans* (Grand Rapids, MI: Eerdmans, 1996), 67; Joseph A. Fitzmyer, *Romans* (New Haven, CT: Yale University Press, 2008), 256; Leon Morris, *The Epistle to the Romans*(Grand Rapids, MI: Eerdmans, 1988), 67.

[24] John A. Witmer, "Romans" in *The Bible Knowledge Commentary*, eds. John F. Walvoord and Roy B. Zuck (Wheaton, IL: Victor Books, 1985), 2:441.

[25] *Euangelion*, "gospel," occurs ten times (Rom 1:1, 9, 16; 2:16; 10:16; 11:28; 14:24; 15:16, 19, 29). The cognate verb *euangelizein*, "to preach the gospel," occurs three times (Rom 1:15; 10:15; 15:20).

to them was not so that they would gain everlasting life. Instead, he wished to aid them in their walk with Christ. Verse 17 is best understood as having the force of a command: "The just by faith shall [should] live."[26] That life is spelled out in Romans 5–8.

The gospel of Christ is a message that can result in believers being delivered from temporal judgment, which Paul calls "the wrath of God" in the verse immediately after vv 16-17 (Rom 1:18).

There is a huge gap before Paul used *sōtēria* again. He did not use it at all in the justification section (Rom 3:21–4:25), which is quite telling.[27] His next use is not until Rom 10:1.

Romans 10:1. Romans 9–11 deal with Paul's concern for Israel. In 10:1 he writes, "Brethren, my heart's desire and prayer to God for Israel is that they may be saved [*estin eis sōtēria*]." The salvation to which Paul refers could be salvation from eternal condemnation, since Paul longed for that for everyone he spoke with. However, since the only other use of *sōtēria* in Romans 10 refers to salvation from God's wrath in this life (see discussion under Rom 10:10) and since the two uses of *sōzō* in Romans 10 also refer to salvation from God's wrath here and now (Rom 10:9, 13), the salvation Paul desires for Israel is their deliverance from God's judgment and their establishment as the blessed nation from which Messiah rules. Compare Rom 11:26.

It should be noted that when the OT speaks of the salvation of Israel, it is referring to Israel's being delivered from God's wrath in this life. Note the parallelism in Jer 23:6a-b, "In His days Judah will be saved, and Israel will dwell safely." To dwell safely is to be saved. The same idea is evident in Jer 31:7b-8a, "Proclaim, give praise, and say, 'O Lord, save Your people, the remnant of Israel!' Behold, I will bring them from the north country, and gather them from the ends of the earth." The regathering and restoration of the Israel is her salvation. So, too, Jer 33:16a, "In those days Judah will be saved, and Jerusalem will dwell safely." The national salvation of Israel is her dwelling safely in her own land without oppression from Gentiles.

---

[26] See Zane C. Hodges, *Romans: Deliverance from Wrath* (Corinth, TX: Grace Evangelical Society, 2013), 37-38.

[27] Paul does not use the verb form, *sōzō*, in the justification section either. His next use of *sōzō* is in Rom 5:9-10 where it is specified as referring to a *future* deliverance *from wrath*: "we shall be saved from wrath through Him." In addition, Paul says in v 10 that "we shall be saved by His life," that is, by our manifesting His life. See Hodges, *Romans*, 140-44.

Most commentators, however, understand this salvation to refer to deliverance from eternal condemnation.[28] However, the other uses of the word in Romans and the immediate context show that deliverance *from temporal wrath* is in view.

Hodges writes, "The term for *deliverance (sōtērian)* is to be taken here consistently with the use throughout the epistle of the word group *sōzō/sōtēria* (see discussions at 1:16; 5:9-10; 8:24; 9:27). Its reference is to rescue from the temporal display of God's anger [against Israel]."[29]

Romans 10:10. Much confusion results from inaccurate exposition of Rom 10:9-10. Commentators who say elsewhere that the sole condition of salvation from eternal condemnation is faith in Christ also say that Rom 10:9-10 teaches that both faith plus confession of Christ are required, though they attempt to downplay that by saying that those are "two parts of the same saving expression."[30] Or they say these "are not two separate steps to salvation. They are chronologically together."[31] Or they explain, "This simple response, surprisingly in light of Paul's stress on faith in this context, is a twofold one: 'if you confess with your mouth' and 'if you believe in your heart.'"[32] Those explanations are contradictory and confusing.

There are two conditions for salvation/deliverance in these verses, one internal (believing in your heart) and one external (confession with your mouth). Since the only condition for justification and regeneration is faith in Christ, the salvation in these verses must not refer to regeneration, but to deliverance from God's wrath in this life, as the other uses of *sōtēria* in Romans attest.

Verse 10 explains v 9: "With the heart one believes unto righteousness [*dikaiosunē*]." That is the justification by faith alone message of Rom 3:21–4:25. The only condition of being made righteous (= justified) is believing. *Dikaiosunē* is the cognate noun associated with the verb *dikaioō* (justify).

---

[28] So, Moo, *Romans*, 631-32; Witmer, *Romans*, 479; Morris, *Romans*, 378.

[29] Hodges, *Romans*, 293.

[30] Morris, *Romans*, 386.

[31] Witmer, *Romans*, 481.

[32] Moo, *Romans*, 657.

However, in order to have salvation from God's wrath in this life, one must not only believe, but he must also confess with his mouth the Lord Jesus.

Confessing the Lord Jesus is understood in various ways. Some commentators suggest that it refers to acknowledging the deity of Christ. Witmer, for example, says it refers to "acknowledging to God that Christ is God."[33] Others say it refers to verbally confessing that "Jesus is Lord." Moo, for instance, writes, "The acclamation of Jesus as Lord is a very early and very central element of Christian confession."[34] Still others suggest that this should be understood not as a confession, but as a prayer. Hodges says, "The response of the mouth should be a confession directly addressing Jesus with the designation 'Lord.' This confession is made in prayer (vv 12-13). This is an appeal to His Lordship for the needed deliverance from divine wrath."[35]

Verses 13-14 support the interpretation that the confession or appeal referred to in Rom 10:9-10 is being made *by a believer, not an unbeliever*, and that the salvation is the deliverance of a believer from God's wrath in this life. In v 13 Paul cites a verse from Joel 2, that reads, "Whoever calls on the name of the Lord shall be saved."

Verse 14 has three rhetorical questions, each of which indicates what comes first. Question 1, "How shall they call on Him in whom they have not believed?" shows that believing in Jesus precedes calling upon Him in prayer. Question 2, "And how shall they believe in Him of whom they have not heard?" demonstrates that hearing about Jesus precedes believing in Him. Question 3, "And how shall they hear without a preacher?" indicates that the preacher must preach about Jesus before people can hear what he says about Him.

Commentators who understand the salvation of Rom 10:13 to refer to the regeneration of unbelievers when they believe find it difficult to explain v 14. Witmer sees a shift: "Previously, to call on the Lord was equated with trusting Him or believing in Him (cf. vv. 11 and 13), but here it follows the believing."[36] But the believing in v 13 is being

---

[33] Witmer, "Romans," 481.

[34] Moo, *Romans*, 658.

[35] Zane C. Hodges, "Romans" in *The Grace New Testament Commentary*, Second Edition, ed. by Robert N. Wilkin(Denton, TX: Grace Evangelical Society, 2019), 334.

[36] Witmer, "Romans," 481.

explained in v14. It does not fit the context to see a shift in the type of person doing the believing.

Moo takes a similar position, saying in reference to v 14, "salvation is a matter of calling on the Lord."[37] In other words, people are saved from eternal condemnation by calling on the Lord. But two paragraphs later, he distinguishes between calling on the Lord and believing in Him: "But people cannot call on the Lord if they do not believe in him."[38] Essentially he is saying that *people cannot believe in the Lord if they do not already believe in the Lord.*

Osborne succinctly explains vv 14-15a: "Thus the order is the sending of the witness, leading to the preaching of the gospel, leading to hearing the message, leading to believing the truth, leading to calling on the Lord."[39] Notice that he indicates that believing precedes calling on the Lord. However, when he speaks about calling on the Lord in vv 12-13, he understands it as referring to initial faith in Christ for salvation *and* later lifelong calling upon Him in prayer and worship. He writes, "Here [v 12] it begins with calling on the Lord in faith for salvation (as in v. 13) and continues with the lifelong calling on the Lord that results."[40] Osborne also says, "Salvation is experienced in the twin responses of confessing and believing."[41] It is hard to understand what he means. In one place he says that calling on the Lord is done in faith, suggesting that is the sole condition. In another he says that salvation is by faith and that calling on the Lord follows faith. In still another he seems to be saying that both responses are needed for one to be saved.

Much confusion would be spared if commentators recognized that *sōtēria* in Romans is deliverance from the wrath of God in this life.

Romans 11:11. This verse is still within the discussion of Israel in Romans 9–11. Paul writes, "I say then, have they stumbled that they should fall? Certainly not! But through their fall, to provoke them to jealousy, salvation has come to the Gentiles." What is this salvation that had come to the Gentiles? It certainly could refer to regeneration. However, nothing in the context suggests that. In fact, the next

---

[37] Moo, *Romans*, 662.

[38] Ibid., 663.

[39] Grant R. Osborne, *Romans* (Downers Grove, IL: InterVarsity, 2004), 274.

[40] Ibid., 273.

[41] Ibid., 270.

verse says, "Now if their fall is riches for the world, and their failure riches for the Gentiles, how much more their fullness!" *Riches for the Gentiles* is parallel to *salvation has come to the Gentiles.*

It is likely that the salvation in Rom 11:11 concerns deliverance from God's wrath in this life. Paul has in mind Gentiles who not only have been justified by faith in Christ (Rom 10:10a), but who also are confessing the Lord Jesus (Rom 10:10b). The result is that they are blessed.

While Moo understands the salvation of the Gentiles as their gaining everlasting life, he concludes his discussion of Rom 11:11 emphasizing the issue of temporal blessings upon Gentiles, which he sees as part of their salvation: "Paul apparently thinks that the Jews, as they see the Gentiles enjoying the messianic blessings promised first of all to them, will want those blessings for themselves."[42]

Romans 13:11. What did Paul mean when he said, "now our salvation is nearer than when we first believed"? Clearly, he was not talking about regeneration, for that does not get any nearer.

Witmer says it refers to "ultimate or final salvation realized at the return of the Savior."[43] Precisely what he means by *ultimate or final salvation* is presumably the time when believers will be raptured and given glorified bodies.

Moo says, "Some Christians might find it puzzling that Paul places 'salvation' in the future for believers. But, in fact, Paul regularly uses 'salvation' and its cognates to denote the believer's final deliverance from sin and death."[44]

Morris adds, "Paul writes elsewhere, 'We eagerly await a Savior from there (i.e., heaven)' (Phil. 3:20), and it is something like that that he is saying here. There is the thought of eager expectation and the thought that the fulness of all that salvation means is yet to come."[45]

Believers will be saved *from the Tribulation wrath* (cf. 1 Thess 5:8-10). Our salvation via the Rapture (1 Thess 4:13-18) is nearer every day which passes. Of course, when that occurs, we will have glorified bodies and a fullness of everlasting life that we've not yet experienced.

---

[42] Moo, *Romans*, 688.

[43] Witmer, "Romans," 491.

[44] Moo, *Romans*, 822.

[45] Morris, *Romans*, 471.

All of the references to salvation in Romans refer to being delivered from God's wrath in the present life.[46]

VI. THREE USES OF *SŌTĒRIA* IN 1-2 THESSALONIANS: DELIVERANCE FROM THE TRIBULATION VIA THE RAPTURE

Paul's two letters to the believers in Thessalonica give more details about the Rapture than any other books in the NT. It should not be surprising, therefore, that the three uses of *sōtēria* in the Thessalonian epistles all refers to escaping the Tribulation wrath via the Rapture.

1 Thessalonians 5:8. Paul's first use of *sōtēria* is in the section of 1 Thessalonians that deals extensively with the Rapture (1 Thess 4:13–5:11). In 1 Thess 5:8, Paul writes, "But let us who are of the day be sober, putting on the breastplate of faith and love, and as a helmet the hope of salvation." Believers are "of the day" in our position. Paul is urging believers to live in keeping with their position. He uses his famous trilogy of faith, hope, and love.

In what sense is "the hope of salvation" a helmet? In the context of 1 Thess 4:13–5:11, the soon anticipated deliverance/salvation is the Rapture (cf. 4:16-18; 5:3-4). Believers already have everlasting life as a present possession (John 5:24). We are eagerly awaiting the Rapture and the return of Christ.

Constable notes,

> The salvation they look forward to is deliverance from the wrath to come when the Lord returns, as is clear from the context. It is not a wishful longing that someday they might be saved eternally. Such a thought is entirely foreign to the New Testament. Followers of Christ have a sure hope; they are not as others who have no hope.[47]

Green takes the same view, writing:

> The hope they enjoyed is specifically linked with their future salvation (cf. Matt. 10:22; 24:13; Mark 13:13;

---

[46] Even in Rom 13:11, the future deliverance of the believer includes escaping wrath since the Tribulation will be a time of great outpouring of God's wrath, and believers will be delivered from the Tribulation via the Rapture.

[47] Thomas L. Constable, "1 Thessalonians" in *The Bible Knowledge Commentary*, ed. by John F. Walvoord and Roy B. Zuck (Wheaton, IL: Victor Books, 1985), 2:706.

Rom. 5:9–10; 1 Cor. 3:15; 2 Tim. 4:18), which here, as
in Romans 5:9–10, is deliverance from the wrath of God,
as the following verse shows. The hope of salvation is not
a vague expectation but rather the settled assurance of
future deliverance (see 1:10; Rom. 8:24).[48]

This understanding is confirmed by the use of *sōtēria* in the very
next verse.

1 Thessalonians 5:9. Verse 9 begins with an explanatory *gar* (*for*):
"For God did not appoint us to wrath, but to obtain salvation
[*sōtēria*] through our Lord Jesus Christ." The wrath in context is the
Tribulation. The way in which believers will obtain salvation from
the Tribulation is by means of the Rapture.

Green comments, "the present concern is with deliverance from
the divine chastisement that will come upon those who rebel against
God's way…The Lord is the one who will deliver believers from the
coming wrath (1:10 and commentary)."[49] Constable adds, "The wrath
of God referred to here clearly refers to the Tribulation; the context
makes this apparent. Deliverance from that wrath is God's appoint-
ment for believers…through the Lord Jesus Christ."[50]

God did not appoint Church Age believers to go through the wrath
that is the Tribulation. He appointed us to escape it via the Rapture.

2 Thessalonians 2:13. After the Rapture occurs, "God will send
them a strong delusion, that they should believe the lie" (2 Thess
2:11). Paul then says that he is "bound to give thanks to God always
for you" because "God from the beginning chose you for salvation
[*sōtēria*] through sanctification by the Spirit and belief in the truth"
(2 Thess 2:13). While those who believe in the Calvinist view of election typically interpret this to be a reference to election to everlasting life,[51] the context does not support such an interpretation. The
Church Age believer has been chosen by God to be saved from the
Tribulation via the Rapture. Compare 1 Thess 5:9.

The end of v 13 needs some comment. Why is this selection for salvation "through sanctification by the Spirit and belief in the truth"?

---

[48] Gene L., Green, *The Letters to the Thessalonians* (Grand Rapids, MI: Eerdmans, 2002), 241.

[49] Ibid., 243.

[50] Constable, "1 Thessalonians," 707.

[51] E.g., Green, *Thessalonians*, 325-26; Constable, "1 Thessalonians," 721.

Paul is giving the divine and human aspects of our selection to be raptured. The word *sanctification* refers to *being set apart*. The Holy Spirit positionally sets the believer apart. This is sometimes called *past sanctification*. That past sanctification occurs at the moment that a person has "belief in the truth" concerning the Lord Jesus Christ.[52]

The three uses of *sōtēria* in 1-2 Thessalonians refer to being delivered from the Tribulation via the Rapture.

VII. SEVEN USES OF *SŌTĒRIA* IN HEBREWS: BECOMING ONE OF CHRIST'S PARTNERS IN THE LIFE TO COME

As is true of nearly every book in the Bible, one's perception of the purpose of Hebrews is vital to interpret it correctly. And that certainly is true of interpreting the word *sōtēria* in Hebrews.

Hebrews 1:14. Being the first use of *sōtēria* in Hebrews, this reference is especially important. The author says that angels are "ministering spirits sent forth to minister for those who will inherit salvation." This salvation is typically understood as *final salvation* or *the completion of our salvation when we are glorified.* Ellingsworth says regarding *sōtēria* in 1:14, "The term is never explained (—> 2:3), and must be considered traditional."[53]

Bruce writes,

> The salvation here spoken of lies in the future; it is yet to be inherited, even if its blessings can already be enjoyed in anticipation. That is to say, it is that eschatological salvation which, in Paul's words, is "nearer to us now than when we first believed" (Rom. 13:11) or, in Peter's words, is "ready to be revealed in the last time" (1 Pet. 1:5).[54]

Rayburn adds, "Throughout Hebrews salvation is viewed in terms of its future consummation. Its present dimensions are not

---

[52] Most commentators understand the salvation here as regeneration and the sanctification as referring to present sanctification. See, for example, Constable, "2 Thessalonians," 721; Green, *Thessalonians*, 326; Gregory K. Beale, 1-2 Thessalonians (Downers Grove, IL: InterVarsity Press, 2003), 226.

[53] Paul Ellingworth, *The Epistle to the Hebrews* (Grand Rapids, MI: Eerdmans, 1993), 133.

[54] F. F. Bruce, *The Epistle to the Hebrews*, rev. ed. (Grand Rapids, MI: Eerdmans, 1964), 25.

emphasized, since they are not immediately relevant to the author's purpose, which is to call his readers to that persevering faith which alone obtains entrance to the heavenly country (10:35–39)."[55]

However, there are contextual clues that this future *sōtēria* here refers to *being Christ's partners* (*metochoi*) in the life to come. Tanner writes, "By salvation, our author is thinking not of our Lord's saving work on the Cross, but a future salvation associated with His Second Coming (emphasized in chap. 1). This is quite clear in light of his use of 'salvation' in 9:28, as well as his explicit mention in 2:5 of 'the world to come.'"[56] He made clear in his comments on Heb 1:9 that he thinks this future salvation refers to being one of Christ's companions in the life to come.[57]

The word *metochoi* (1:9) refers to *partners* in Luke 5:7. It is used in Heb 3:14 in an eschatological sense: "For we have become partakers [*metochoi*] of Christ if we hold fast the beginning of our confidence to the end." To be Christ's partner in the life to come one must hold fast to the end of his life (cf. 1 Cor 15:2; 2 Tim 2:12; Rev 2:26). Everlasting life is secure the moment one believes in Christ (John 3:16; 5:24; 6:35; 11:26). But future partnership with Christ requires endurance (cf. 2 Tim 2:12; Rev 2:26).

Angels are not sent out by God to help all believers. He sends them out to help believers *who are walking in fellowship*, those who are Christ's partners and will remain so forever if they hold fast in their Christian experience.

Hebrews 2:3. This second use of *sōtēria* in Hebrews helps explain the first. It is within the first warning passage in Hebrews (2:1-4). The author asks, "how shall we escape if we neglect so great a salvation…?" The salvation (*sōtēria*) of which he is speaking is the same as that in Heb 1:14.

Since most commentators understand the salvation in Heb 1:14 to refer to entering Christ's eschatological kingdom, they also understand

[55] Robert S. Rayburn, "Hebrews" in *Evangelical Commentary on the Bible* (Grand Rapids, MI: Baker Book House, 1995), 3:1133.

[56] J. Paul Tanner, "The Epistle to the Hebrews" in *The Grace New Testament Commentary*, ed. by Robert N. Wilkin (Denton, TX: Grace Evangelical Society, 2010), 2:1036.

[57] Ibid.: "[the OT citation in 1:9] mentions the king's 'companions' (*metochous*), a term he later applies to believers who participate in the heavenly calling to the New Jerusalem of the New Covenant." See also, Zane C. Hodges, "Hebrews" in *The Bible Knowledge Commentary*, ed. by John F. Walvoord and Roy B. Zuck (Wheaton, IL: Victor Books, 1985), 2:782.

sōtēria here in that way. Ellingworth says, "the message about Christ is an event which brings salvation to those who believe."[58] Bruce writes,

> But the great salvation proclaimed in the gospel was brought to earth by no angel, but by the Son of God himself. To treat it lightly, therefore, must expose one to sanctions even more awful than those which safeguarded the law...This is the first of several places in the epistle where an inference is drawn a fortiori from law to gospel.[59]

However, the first-person plural shows that the author is speaking to believers about something bad that could happen to them if they continue to "drift away" (2:1). While believers cannot lose everlasting life (Heb 10:10, 14), they can lose the opportunity to be Christ's partners, co-rulers, in the life to come (Heb 3:14).

Hebrews 2:10. In the third use of *sōtēria* in Hebrews, Jesus is called, "the captain of their salvation." He was "made perfect [or, *made complete*] through sufferings." The Lord Jesus was sent to suffer and then to die. He would not finish the work the Father sent Him to do until He died on the cross. The night before the cross, He said, "Now My soul is troubled, and what shall I say? 'Father, save Me from this hour'? But for this purpose, I came to this hour" (John 12:27).

Many commentators understand the author to be saying that Jesus is our Savior. Bruce, for example, writes, "He is the Savior who blazed the trail of salvation...As His people's representative and forerunner He has now entered into the presence of God to secure their entry there."[60]

However, the text says that He is "the captain of [the] salvation" *of all believers who follow Him on the path of suffering* (cf. Matt 16:24-28; Heb 5:9). Only by following Him on that path will we become His partners in the life to come. This is not a promise to all believers.

It should be noted that He is leading believers who follow Him "to glory." In Hebrews and in this context future glory is reserved for enduring believers only. Christ's partners will share in His rule and in His glory. Tanner comments,

> The word *glory* recalls Psalm 8 again (see Heb 2:7) and how Christ experienced glory in resurrection and exaltation.

[58] Ellingworth, *Hebrews*, 141.
[59] Bruce, *Hebrews*, 29.
[60] Bruce, *Hebrews*, 43.

To bring *many sons to glory* looks at God's plan for believers also to share in glory, as Christ Himself did after
successfully completing His earthly pilgrimage. Because
of their faith in Him, they will eventually receive the glory
of resurrection and (if they do not neglect the "so great a
salvation") a sharing in the glorious reign and dominion
of the Son. The latter privilege is conditional in light of
2:1–4 (cf. 4:1ff).[61]

Hebrews 5:9. This is the fourth use of *sōtēria* in Hebrews and the
first use since Heb 2:10. The author, speaking of Jesus, says, "And
having been perfected, He became the author of eternal salvation
to all who obey Him…" To refer to Him as "the author of eternal
salvation" is similar to the previous reference to Him as "the captain
of their salvation." As with chap. 2, the author indicates that He will
only give this *salvation* to those "who obey Him."

This is the only use of the expression *eternal salvation* in the entire
NT.[62] And it is conditioned not upon faith, but upon obedience.

Hughes says, without explanation, "Here again, then, they are being
reminded, as previously they have more forcefully been reminded (cf.
2:3; 3:12ff.; 4:11), that this great salvation belongs only to those who
persevere in obedience to Christ."[63] Bruce takes the same view, once
again without an explanation as to how this harmonizes with salvation by faith alone in over a hundred NT verses.[64] He does note,
however, that the author is linking the obedience of Christ in Heb
5:8 to the obedience to those whom He will give eternal salvation.[65]

Once it is recognized that this salvation is obtained by obedience
and not by faith, it should be obvious that this salvation does not
refer to regeneration and escaping eternal condemnation since that is
conditioned upon faith alone, not obedience.

Tanner gives four reasons why *"eternal salvation* in this verse does
not refer to redemption from sin based on Christ's atonement:

---

[61] Tanner, "Hebrews," 1039.

[62] It is found once in the OT in Isa 45:17. There it refers to the future reign of the Messiah and of Israel over all the countries of the world.

[63] Philip Edgcumbe Hughes, *A Commentary on the Epistle to the Hebrews* (Grand Rapids, MI: Eerdmans, 1977), 188.

[64] Bruce, *Hebrews*, 105-106.

[65] Ibid.

First, of seven occurrences of "salvation" in Hebrews... not once does it clearly mean *salvation from sin*...Second, Christ's experience in 5:7-8 is meant to parallel that of believers...Third, the context has not been talking about a sinner's need for salvation from sin...Fourth, the obedience mentioned in 5:9 must be seen in light of the preceding verse. The word "obey" in v 9 (from *hupakouō*) is clearly associated with the word "obedience" in v 8 (from the related noun, *hupokoē*).[66]

Tanner goes on to suggest that this *eternal salvation* refers to "shar[ing] in Christ's inheritance and reign[ing] with Him."[67] Hodges agrees, writing,

[This eternal salvation] should not be confused with the acquisition of eternal life which is conditioned not on obedience but on faith (cf. John 3:16, etc.). Once again, the author had in mind final deliverance from and victory over all enemies and the consequent enjoyment of the "glory" of the many sons and daughters. This kind of salvation is explicitly contingent on obedience and indeed on an obedience modeled after that of Jesus who also suffered.[68]

Hebrews 6:9. After giving the third warning (Heb 5:11–6:8), the author then says in this fifth use of *sōtēria* that he is confident that the readers will not fall away, but that they would do well concerning "things that accompany salvation." The things which the author is confident they will continue to do are the good works that flow from the Word of God when a believer receives it (Heb 6:7).

The *salvation* of which the author speaks is once again often seen as referring to regeneration. Bruce writes, "the fruits of righteousness had beyond all question manifested themselves in their lives. Those fruits, being the natural concomitants of salvation, bore witness that the people in whom they appeared were genuine heirs of salvation."[69] Koester agrees: "The sharpness of the reproof in 5:11–6:3 and of the warning in 6:4-8 does not mean that the author has lost hope for the listeners. His words are designed to motivate listeners to persevere,

---

[66] Tanner, *Hebrews*, 1050.

[67] Ibid.

[68] Zane C. Hodges, "Hebrews" in *The Bible Knowledge Commentary*, vol. 2, ed. by John F. Walvoord and Roy B. Zuck (Wheaton, IL: Victor Books, 1985), 792.

[69] Bruce, *Hebrews*, 126.

not to drive them to despair of God."[70] In his view only those who persevere will enter Christ's kingdom.[71]

However, there is nothing in 6:4-8 that implies that the eternal destiny of anyone who fails to persevere is being threatened. The warning, like all the warnings in Hebrews, concerns temporal judgment and the possibility of missing out on ruling with Christ in the life to come. The illustration of Heb 6:7-8 is that we burn the worthless overgrowth of fields. The field represents the believer. His worthless overgrowth represents works that are burned. But the field remains. There is no reason to see *salvation* in Heb 6:9 as anything other than what it has been in the whole book thus far, that is, becoming Christ's partners in the life to come.[72]

Hebrews 9:28. In his sixth use of *sōtēria*, the author says that Christ "was offered once to bear the sins of many" during His first coming. Then when he refers to Christ's Second Coming, he brings in the theme of future salvation for faithful believers: "To those who eagerly wait for Him He will appear a second time, apart from sin, for salvation."

Bruce represents most commentators who see this future salvation as entering Christ's kingdom: "So our author thinks of Jesus as going into the heavenly holy of holies, to reappear one day in order to confirm finally to his people the salvation which his perfect offering has procured for them."[73] A bit later he makes clear that he interprets salvation in Hebrews to require perseverance: "All the blessings which he [Jesus] won for his people at His first appearing will be theirs to enjoy in perpetual fulness at His second appearing. Therefore, let them not grow faint and weary but persevere in patience and faith."[74]

Not all believers will receive this future salvation. It is only "those who eagerly wait for Him." Compare 2 Tim 4:8 where Paul says that the Lord, the righteous Judge, will give "the crown of righteousness" to him "on that Day [the Judgment Seat of Christ], and not to me

---

[70] Craig R. Koester, *Hebrews* (New Haven, CT: Yale University Press, 2008), 316.

[71] Koester's discussion of 3:14 as well as 6:11-12 confirms that he understands the author of Hebrews to be saying that only those who persevere in the faith will enter Christ's kingdom.

[72] See J. Paul Tanner, "But If It Yields Thorns and Thistles: An Exposition of Hebrews 5:11–6:12," *JOTGES* (Spring 2001): 19-42.

[73] Bruce, *Hebrews,* 224.

[74] Ibid.

only but also to all who have loved His appearing." The salvation of Heb 9:28 is the same as it has been in the entire letter. It is the future selection by Christ to be one of His partners in His kingdom. As Hodges writes,

> Deftly the author implied that "those who are waiting for Him" constitute a smaller circle than those whom His death has benefited. They are, as all his previous exhortations reveal, the ones who "hold firmly till the end the confidence we had at first" (3:14). The "salvation" He will bring them at His second coming will be the "eternal inheritance" of which they are heirs (cf. 9:15; 1:14).[75]

Hebrews 11:7. This seventh and final use of *sōtēria* is a bit of an outlier. The author says, "By faith Noah, being divinely warned of things not yet seen, moved with godly fear, prepared an ark for the saving of his household, by which he condemned the world and became heir of the righteousness which is according to faith." The salvation here refers to the physical salvation of Noah and his family from death in the flood.

Ellingworth represents the view of most commentators on salvation in Hebrews in general and Heb 11:7 in particular:

> Elsewhere in Hebrews (—> 1:14; 2:3, 10; 5:9) the reference is to eternal salvation, connected as here with obedience in 6:9; 9:28; only here is there reference to a temporal escape from drowning, and even here the wider implications are perhaps not entirely absent, since Noah's rescue from the flood is an essential link in God's purpose for his people.[76]

Hodges ties his understanding of Heb 11:7 to his understanding that salvation in the entire letter refers to becoming Christ's partners in the life to come:

> That God does reward those who seek Him is suggested by the career of Noah, who became an heir of righteousness by faith. What he inherited was, in fact, the new world after the Flood as the readers might inherit "the world to come" (cf. 2:5). The reference here to Noah saving his household recalls the writer's stress on a Christian's

---

[75] Zane C. Hodges, "Hebrews" in *The Bible Knowledge Commentary*, ed. by John F. Walvoord and Roy B. Zuck (Wheaton, IL: Victor Books, 1985), 2:803.

[76] Ellingworth, *Hebrews*, 579.

salvation-inheritance. It further suggests that a man's personal faith can be fruitful in his family, as they share it together.[77]

Except for the one reference to deliverance from death in Heb 11:7, all the uses of *sōtēria* in Hebrews refer to being Christ's partners in the life to come. And, as Hodges suggests, even that reference may allude to ruling with Christ in the world to come. That privilege will not be for all believers, but only for those who endure to the end of their Christian lives in faith and good works.

CONCLUSION

Doing word studies is a vital aspect of hermeneutics. We cannot understand the Bible correctly unless we understand the meaning of key Biblical terms. That is certainly true of the words *sōtēria* and *sōzō*. Often new or untaught believers routinely understand the words *salvation* and *save* to refer to escaping eternal condemnation. That results in terrible confusion.

In some books of the Bible, these words are used in precisely the same sense in all or nearly all of their uses. Once one grasps that fact, the interpretation of the books opens up. Hebrews, Romans, Philippians, James, and 1-2 Thessalonians are all examples of cases in which the authors use *sōtēria* and *sōzō* with one uniform sense (and not the sense of salvation from eternal condemnation).

The reader is urged to do this study for himself. Check out all the uses of *sōtēria* and *sōzō* in these five books, and the entire NT.

---

[77] Hodges, "Hebrews," 808.

THE TABLE OF THE LORD, PART 2

ERIC SVENDSEN[1]

I. THE ALLEGED SEPARATION OF THE EUCHARIST FROM THE COMMON MEAL

In 1 Corinthians 11, Paul addresses the Lord's Supper as it relates to the unity within the assembly of the Corinthians. It is evident from Paul's words in this passage that the Corinthians were partaking of an entire meal, not just the bread and wine. As we have already pointed out, very few dispute this.[2] What is disputed, however, is the precise relationship between the Lord's Supper and the Corinthians' meal, and whether Paul in this passage gives any indication that he wants the Corinthians to put an end to their practice of eating a meal together or whether he wants them to continue. To find the answers to these questions it will be helpful to look at the tradition that Paul received about the Supper, and then to reexamine the so-called "Pauline Precedent."

A. Paul's Concept of "The Lord's Supper"

The first step in deciding about the ongoing relevance of the meal-aspect of the Supper is to determine just what Paul means by the title "Lord's Supper" in 1 Cor 11:20. This title, *kuriakon deipnon*, occurs only here in the NT. The word *kuriakon* means roughly "belonging to the Lord." In this case the title means "the supper belonging to the Lord."[3] Yet just what is this "supper"? Is Paul here referring to the

---

[1] Editor's Note: This article was part of a booklet written by the author in 1996. It was published by the New Testament Restoration Foundation in Atlanta, GA. The plan is to publish the booklet in three parts in this journal. This is part 2, with part 1 having appeared in the Spring 2021 Journal. Due to length constraints, some sections are omitted, including some explanations found in footnotes. There are also format changes, such as the numbering of sections and the transliteration of Greek words. Regarding short form footnotes here in part 2, see part 1 for long form publication information. The full booklet, in its original format, can be found at: https://comingintheclouds.org/wpclouds7/wp-content/uploads/2011/03/the_table_of_lord_communion_Lords_supper.pdf. Used by permission.

[2] F. F. Bruce, *First and Second Corinthians* (London: Oliphants, 1971), 110.

[3] C. K. Barrett, *A Commentary on the First Epistle to the Corinthians* (New York: Harper

meal of the Corinthians, of which the bread and wine are dominant features, or is he referring to the bread and wine alone? Put another way, could Paul have referred to the bread and wine as a "supper" apart from the meal?

It is an interesting fact that every other instance of "supper" in the NT refers to nothing less than a full meal, and in many (arguably, all) cases it refers to a banquet or feast. It would be odd in light of this to maintain that Paul has in mind the so-called "elements" (i.e., the bread and wine)—apart from the meal— when he refers to the *kuriakon deipnon*. On the contrary, what Paul calls the "Lord's Supper" is itself the meal with the bread and wine.[4] The bread and wine by themselves can no more be called the Lord's Supper than the meal without the bread and wine. Any attempt to view *kuriakon deipnon* as a title for a symbolic supper is refuted on the grounds that the Corinthians themselves were not partaking of a symbolic supper but rather a real supper.[5] This seems clear from Paul's corrective of their abuses: "When you come together, it is not the Lord's Supper you eat, for as you eat, each of you goes ahead without waiting for anybody else. One remains hungry, another gets drunk" (1 Cor 11:21-22).

B. The Order of the Lord's Supper in Paul

One way to determine whether or not Paul considered the meal-aspect of the Lord's Supper to be a crucial part of the Supper is to take a closer look at the tradition he received about the Supper. Paul tells us about this tradition in 1 Cor 11:23-26:

> For I received from the Lord what I also passed on to you: The Lord Jesus, on the night he was betrayed, took bread, and when he had given thanks, he broke it and said, "This is my body, which is for you; do this in remembrance of me." In the same way, after supper he took the cup, saying, "This cup is the new covenant in my blood; do this, whenever you drink it, in remembrance of me." For whenever you eat this bread and drink this cup, you proclaim the Lord's death until he comes.

& Row, 1968), 262.

[4] Michael J. Townsend, "Exit the Agape?" *ExpT* 90 (1978-79): 358.

[5] H. R. Gummey, "Lord's Supper," *The International Standard Bible Encyclopedia* (Grand Rapids: Eerdmans, 1979-88), 1923.

Several important points can be made about Paul's words here. First, the order of consumption is, for Paul, bread/supper—cup. Paul does not say when they began eating the meal, only that the cup came after. The "cup" referred to here is likely the "cup of blessing" which in Jewish custom was consumed after eating, since, as Fee has noted, this phrase was in use as "a technical term for the final blessing offered at the end of the meal."[6] Paul, in fact, uses this phrase for the cup of the Lord's Supper in 1 Cor 10:16.

Second, we may assume since Paul makes the point that the cup was distributed *after* supper, that the saying about the bread took place either immediately before the meal (to initiate the meal) or during the meal. It is therefore likely that, in Paul's Lord's Supper tradition, the loaf is distributed at the beginning or during the meal and the cup follows the meal. What is significant about this order is the inclusion of the mention of an actual meal within the tradition itself. Why does Paul include this? Doubtless there were many things that took place at the Last Supper that are not included in any of the Lord's Supper traditions. Yet Paul speaks of the meal-aspect ("after supper") as an integral part of his tradition.[7] This passing reference does not bespeak the unimportance of the meal, but rather the *assumption* that the meal is to be included in the practice of the Lord's Supper.[8] Moreover, it was commonplace in the first century to initiate a meal by breaking bread. This fact alone argues strongly that the breaking of bread at the Lord's Supper *assumes* the initiation of an actual meal.

Third, none of the Synoptic accounts contradicts Paul's order here. Matthew and Mark place the saying about the bread "while they were eating," whereas Luke is silent in this regard. While Luke's silence may be taken to mean that they were not yet eating when Jesus distributed the bread, it may also be taken to mean that Luke assumes they were already eating. In any case, as has already been pointed out in a previous chapter,[9] Paul is, strictly speaking, the only one of the

---

[6] Fee, 468. So also Barrett, 231.

[7] The early church must have understood the meal-aspect to be an integral part of the Lord's Supper in order to have included this phrase; for as even Fee (554) concedes, it forms an "otherwise unnecessary role in the tradition."

[8] As Theissen (152) notes, "The formula presumes that there is a meal between the word over the bread and that spoken over the cup. One gets to the cup *after the supper*" (italics his). See also Townsend, 357; Ringe, 62; and Bornkamm, 155.

[9] Part 1 of this series is in the Spring 2021 edition of the *JOTGES*.

four whose primary purpose for including this tradition is to establish the correct practice of the Supper. To that extent, Paul's order must be seen as more relevant to the actual practice of the early church than the Synoptic accounts.

It should be mentioned here that Marshall objects to the idea that the early church followed the order of the Last Supper meal since "it ignores the fact that what Paul cited was not an account of what the church ought to do but a description of what Jesus did... the church's meal was not a Passover meal."[10] While it is true that the church's meal was not a Passover, it seems difficult to imagine why Paul's tradition, which Marshall regards as a liturgical account, would not be formulated in such a way as to indicate the order of the proceedings which the church was to follow. Indeed, what reason is there to assume that the order would be otherwise? In light of this, it seems best to view Paul's tradition of the Supper as that which is to be reflected by the practice of the church. As Theissen notes:

> It is unthinkable that Paul would quote a sacred, cultic formula, expressly state that he received it in just this and no other form, yet at the same time tacitly suppose that its order is not to be followed...If he wants to bring about some order [1 Co 11:34], he cannot possibly repeat obsolete instructions.[11]

Fourth, the question must again be asked: What does Paul mean by "supper" in this passage? Does he have in mind here a symbolic supper consisting only of bread and wine? Or, does he have in mind an actual meal as would be expected of one recalling the events of the Last Supper of the Lord and his disciples? Paul uses the same word (*deipnon*) that he used in v. 20 (although in the verbal form this time). It seems then that Paul sees the meal-aspect as part of his tradition, and that the meal with the bread and cup form the Lord's Supper.

C. The "Pauline Precedent" Reexamined

Many who concede that the Corinthians were, in fact, partaking of an actual meal have postulated that Paul's purpose for writing this

---

[10] Marshall, *Last Supper and Lord's Supper*, 111.
[11] Theissen, 152.

pericope is to put an end to the meal-aspect.[12] This is alternatively based on the assumption that Paul sees this meal as the source of the Corinthians' divisions,[13] or that Paul does not view the meal as an essential aspect of the Lord's Supper to begin with,[14] or a combination of both.[15] Evidence that can be adduced in favor of the view that Paul is here putting an end to the meal-aspect of the Lord's Supper includes: (1) Paul tells the Corinthians that their meal is not the Lord's Supper (v 20) and that the Lord's Supper consists only of the bread and cup to which Paul refers extensively in verses 23-28; (2) Paul implies that he wants them to cease practice of the meal-aspect by his statement, "Don't you have homes to eat and drink in?" (v 22); and (3) Paul ends this section with the words "if anyone is hungry, he should eat at home, so that when you meet together it may not result in judgment" (v 34). Here, it is argued, is the Pauline Precedent that initiated the cessation of the meal-aspect of the Lord's Supper once and for all.[16]

Against point (1) it may be noted that the seeming emphasis Paul places on the bread and cup in verses 23-28 is not intended to *de*-emphasize the importance of the meal-aspect. Even Fee (who subscribes to the cessationist view of the meal-aspect) concedes this point: "The context makes it clear that 'to eat the bread and drink the cup of the Lord' means simply to participate in the meal known as the Lord's Supper. Paul is not trying to give special emphasis to the bread and

---

[12] So, e.g., Kasper (131-32), "The repetition of the special words and gestures of Jesus also came to be separated; [sic] at a very early stage, from the normal 'full meal.' This is already evident with Paul, in 1 Cor. 11:17-34."

[13] So Héring, 113. See also B. Klappert, "Lord's Supper," *The New International Dictionary of New Testament Theology*, vol. 2, ed. C. Brown (Grand Rapids: Zondervan/Exeter: Paternoster, 1975—78), 530, "the separation of the meal from the Lord's Supper is also assumed in 1 Cor. 11. It is here that the direct cause of the Corinthian abuse lies."

[14] So Grosheide, 268. See also Frank C. Senn ("The Lord's Supper, Not the Passover Seder," *Worship* 60 [1986]: 366) who says, "If the Lord's presence is attached to the bread and cup, the rest of the meal is superfluous...The Lord's Supper is a ritual meal; it need not be an actual meal."

[15] So, e.g., Conzelmann (195) who, although seeing the Lord's Supper in Corinth as a "real meal," nevertheless views Paul's corrective as an attempt "to separate the sacrament from satisfaction of hunger" so that the Supper "thereby loses its character of 'agape.'" According to Conzelmann, "in this way the church celebration becomes a pure celebration of the Sacrament," ibid.

[16] So Higgins, 60-61, 71; and F. V. Filson, *A New Testament History: The Story of the Emerging Church* (Philadelphia: Westminster, 1964), 252.

wine per se."[17] In addition, Paul's statement "it is not the *Lord's* Supper you eat" (v 20) is not intended to deny that the Lord's Supper consists of a meal; rather that the Corinthian meal, at one time regarded as the Lord's Supper, can no longer be regarded as such because of the abuses associated with it. This is clear from Paul's explanation of his statement in the very next verse: "*for* as you eat, each of you goes ahead without waiting for anybody else. One remains hungry, another gets drunk" (v 21). In other words, what would, under normal conditions, be the *Lord's* Supper, the Corinthians, by their divisions, have turned into their *own* Supper. Paul is not here attempting to separate the meal from the bread and wine; rather whatever points he makes about the meal are applied equally to the bread and cup (vv 29-30).

Against point (2) above we may again question the assumptions regarding Paul's intent. Barrett is right when he notes about verse 22:

> On the surface this seems to imply that ordinary, non-cultic eating and drinking should be done at home, contradicting the inference drawn above [from vv. 20-21] that the Corinthian supper included an ordinary meal. But Paul's point is that, if the rich wish to eat and drink on their own, enjoying better food than their poorer brothers, they should do this at home; if they cannot wait for others (verse 33), if they must indulge to excess, *they can at least keep the church's common meal free from practices that can only bring discredit upon it.*[18] (Italics mine)

This same observation may be made against point (3) above. There it is argued that Paul's closing words for this section ("if anyone is hungry, he should eat at home," v 34) imply Paul's desire that the meal-aspect of the Lord's Supper should cease. Yet, as Barrett notes above about verse 22, Paul's concern is to put an end, not to the meal itself, but to the abuses that accompanied the meal. This seems clear on two counts. First, Paul uses the singular pronoun and the singular imperative in this verse—lit., "if any*one* is hungry, let *him* eat at home"—not the plural. This suggests strongly that Paul's point is simply that if any *individual* cannot restrain himself from eating the Supper before the poor arrive, then that individual should eat

---

[17] Fee, 560.

[18] Barrett, 263.

something at home so that he won't be tempted to hoard that which rightly belongs to the entire body. Second, the verse that immediately precedes verse 34 seems to preclude any notion that Paul here intends to put an end to the meal-aspect: "So then, my brothers, when you come together to eat, wait for each other," (v 33). If Paul means to abolish the meal-aspect of the Lord's Supper then it is odd that he would make a closing statement which assumes that the Corinthians will continue the meal as they have been (minus, of course, the abuses). Indeed, the only modification of the Supper that interests Paul is that the Corinthians "wait for each other" so that all may partake of the meal together.[19]

II. THE *AGAPE* IN JUDE 12

Tucked away in Jude's short epistle is a singular reference to the *Agape* (Jude 12, *agapais*, often translated as "love feasts"). There may also be a reference to this "feast" in 2 Pet 2:13 ("feasting with you"). This feast in Jude (as well as in Peter) is included as a passing reference (not unlike Paul's teaching on the bread and cup in 1 Cor 10:16-17). However, as with Paul, we may detect certain assumptions on the part of Jude for including it in the first place. It will be helpful first to survey the context in which this reference is found.

Jude's letter is one of urgency; that much is evident from his greeting. Although he had originally planned to write a general letter dealing with issues of salvation, he felt constrained to write instead to warn his readers about certain heretics who had infiltrated the church (vv 3-4). He compares these heretics to some of the OT villains that incurred God's judgment, including the rabble that Moses had to deal with, fallen angels, and the men of Sodom and Gomorrah (vv 5-7). Beginning then in verse 8, Jude sets out to make application to the current heretics. They "pollute their own bodies, reject authority and slander celestial beings" (v 8). They are compared, not only to the foregoing villains, but to Cain, Balaam, and Korah as well (v 11). It is in this context that Jude mentions the *Agape*: "These men are blemishes at your love feasts, eating with you without the slightest qualm" (v 12). The question is: Just what is this *Agape*?

---

[19] Cf. Marshall, *Last Supper and Lord's Supper*, 110; Bornkamm, 129, 155; and Winter, 73.

A. Common Meal or Lord's Supper?

On a purely contextual level, it seems evident that Jude is first referring to a common meal. Although the word *agapais* is literally "loves," it is closely connected by Jude to the participle form of "feast together" (*suneuōchoumenoi*), which occurs only in Jude 12 and in 2 Pet 2:13. For this reason, and since Jude and Peter cite identical thematic content, it seems safe to assume that both writers have the same thing in mind. Aside from this evidence (and the witness of the early church in the post-apostolic era, to which we will turn shortly), no scholar seems to question that Jude is using *agapais* as a term for a Christian feast. The disagreement is over whether it is a term that designates *merely* a common meal, or is, in fact, a synonym for the Lord's Supper.

Some scholars view Jude's reference here as nothing more than a common fellowship meal.[20] This is not a widely held view, however, and most scholars have adopted the view that Jude is here referring to none other than the Lord's Supper itself.[21] In Townsend's words:

> There is nothing…to suggest that this excludes the Eucharist itself…[and]…there seems [to be] no good reason why *agapais* here should not fulfill the same function as *kuriakon deipnon* does in 1 Cor 11:20, where, as we have seen, it refers to the total complex of events, i.e., the Eucharist in its normal common-meal setting…It is prima facie unlikely…that Jude 12 should refer to an Agape distinct from the Eucharist.[22]

With this Marshall agrees when he notes: "There is nothing to suggest that the love feast was a separate kind of meal from the Lord's Supper, and it seems more probable that these were two different names for the same occasion."[23] It is indeed more difficult to

---

[20] So Simon Kistemaker, *Peter and Jude* (Grand Rapids: Baker Book House, 1987), 392; and W. Gunther and H. G. Link, "Love," *NIDNTT*, vol. 2, 547; and, to some extent, J. N. D. Kelly, *A Commentary on the Epistles of Peter and Jude*, HNTC (San Francisco: Harper and Row, 1969), 269-70.

[21] Included here, among many others, are Green (188-89); Townsend (360); Marshall, *Last Supper and Lord's Supper*, 110; Higgins (60), C. Spicq, *Agape in the New Testament* (St. Louis: B. Herder Book Co., 1965), 370; R. Bauckham, *Jude, 2 Peter*, WBC 50 (Waco, TX: Word, 1983), 84; and Edwin Blum "Jude," *EBC*, 392.

[22] Townsend, 360.

[23] Marshall, *Last Supper and Lord's Supper*, 110.

understand Jude's anxiety about ungodly men partaking of this meal if it is not the Lord's Supper and if it does not include the Eucharist. It seems best, therefore, to view Jude's *Agape* as the Lord's Supper itself.

B. Jude's Relevance to the Issue

Jude's relevance to the issue of the common meal in the Lord's Supper is twofold: (1) Jude offers non-Pauline corroboration about the Supper; and (2) he reveals the importance of the Supper via a specialized term. We shall elaborate on each of these points in turn.

C. Non-Pauline Corroboration

The fact that Jude, in writing to his churches, can refer to a church practice that is similar to Paul's is revealing in that it implies the universality of this practice. Higgins assumes that this meal-aspect of the Lord's Supper was practiced universally by the church when he says, "The custom at Corinth, *as elsewhere*, was for the special eucharistic partaking of bread and wine to take place during the course of a meal"[24] (italics mine). Not only was this participation in a eucharistic common meal "likely the practice of every Pauline church,"[25]it was, as Jude 12 indicates, likely the practice of every apostolic church. In Spicq's view the church held the *Agape* in order to "reproduce as exactly as possible the circumstances that surrounded the institution of the Eucharist."[26]It would be odd in light of this to maintain that this meal was confined to Pauline churches alone; for the meaning and significance of the Last Supper applies equally to all churches. It seems best then to conclude that the *Agape* in Jude corroborates the Lord's Supper in Paul as a common meal which served as a setting for the bread and cup of the Eucharist, and which was practiced universally by the apostolic church.

D. Agape as a Specialized Term

One other indication of the universality of the *Agape* may be seen in the name itself. While the mere practice of the *Agape* by the early

---

[24] Higgins, 60.

[25] G. B. Caird, *The Apostolic Age* (London: Duckworth, 1975), 52.

[26] Spicq, 370.

church cannot be seen as the determining factor in whether or not this practice was considered normative,[27] it seems likely that since this practice had been given a special name it was indeed considered a normative practice by the apostolic church itself. This is the basis upon which Bauckham[28] and Lincoln[29] view Sunday as the normative day of meeting for the church. Bauckham notes, for instance, that the regular, consistent practice of meeting on Sunday coupled with the use of the specialized term, Lord's Day, "gives that custom the stamp of canonical authority."[30] With this Lincoln concurs:

> That the first day of the week was given the title Lord's Day suggests a matter of far greater import than convenience or practicality...True, the designation "Lord's Day" in [Rev 1:10] is incidental rather than being part of the primary didactic intent of the writer, but we are not using this passing reference in order to establish a precedent but to show that a precedent had already been set in the practice of at least John's churches and evidently met with his approval. So in the case of worship on the first day of the week we have a pattern that is repeated in the New Testament, and as is shown by Revelation 1:10, the pattern had become established.[31]

What can be said here about the "Lord's Day" applies with equal force to the "Lord's Supper/*Agape*." Indeed, we may claim even more evidence for a normative practice of this meal since much more is said about it in the NT than about the Lord's Day. Moreover, as Lincoln has noted, John alone uses the title Lord's Day. Yet, as Lincoln further notes:

> Although we have evidence for this pattern from only some parts of the early church, its rationale is not one that was applicable only to those parts or indeed applicable only to the early church period but one that remains applicable throughout the church's life. Hence the practice

---

[27] Other factors must be weighed as well, including the underlying theology of the practice, the way in which the practice is presented by the NT writers, and the extent to which the practice is distinct from the practices of the surrounding culture and other religious groups.

[28] Bauckham, "The Lord's Day," 221-50.

[29] Lincoln, 343-412.

[30] Bauckham, "The Lord's Day," 240.

[31] Lincoln, 387-88.

of Sunday worship can be said to be not merely one that recommends itself because it bears the mark of antiquity but one that, though not directly commanded, lays high claim to bearing the mark of canonical authority.[32]

This is likewise true in the case of the *Agape*. Although Jude alone uses this title, Paul, as we have seen, refers to the same meal and calls it the Lord's Supper. Neither writer gives a direct command to adhere to this practice of holding a meal; yet, as in the case of John and the Lord's Day, each writer assumes, by virtue of the use of a specialized name, that the practice is an established, universal custom. Moreover, as with the Lord's Day, the "rationale" of the meal (inasmuch as it is part and parcel of the tradition that was handed down to Paul from the other Apostles, and inasmuch as it is a "reproduction" of the Last Supper[33]) must apply equally and in the same way to all churches.

III. THE TESTIMONY OF EARLY CHURCH HISTORY

By the middle of the second century the Eucharist and the accompanying meal stand as separate ceremonies, presumably to keep the Eucharist from becoming profaned by the participation of unbelievers.[34] Jeremias thinks that the origin of this separation can be traced back to "the time of Paul"[35] and was done to safeguard the Eucharist from the unbaptized. However, while Jeremias' rationale for this separation is no doubt valid, Townsend is probably correct in ascribing the separation to the post-apostolic period.[36] As Townsend notes:

> At the earliest stage of the tradition however, there is no evidence that such a procedure [of separating the Eucharist from the *Agape*] was envisaged. We must be extremely careful not to read back into the NT from the undoubted practice of the second and subsequent Christian centuries.[37]

---

[32] Ibid., 388.

[33] Spicq, 370.

[34] J. Jeremias, *The Eucharistic Words of Jesus* (London: SCM, 1966), 116, 132-33

[35] Ibid., 133.

[36] Townsend, 359.

[37] Ibid., 360.

This separation then most likely occurred during the second century; yet throughout the NT period and even beyond "Christians met together to hold common meals that were more than a token reception of bread and wine."[38] Marshall is no doubt right in his belief that whatever may have been the relationship between the Eucharist and the common meal in later times, "they belonged together in New Testament times."[39] Although we cannot know with certainty the exact date at which this separation occurred, we can nevertheless pinpoint the general period by examining some of the writings of the second century.

A. Tertullian

Although Tertullian does not make the express connection between the Eucharist and the *Agape*, we know with certainty that the *Agape* was still in practice during his time. In his *Apology*, Tertullian describes for us a meeting of the early church during an *Agape*.[40] His thrust is clearly to defend the Christian feast against false accusations of extravagance. Tertullian insists that at this feast Christians eat and drink as "temperate people," eating only as much as satisfies hunger and drinking only as much as needed to quench thirst. Through it all, Tertullian gives no indication that there would be cessation of partaking of this meal. On the contrary, he insists that it involves nothing that can be considered illegal and characterizes the feast as a "rule of life" for Christians. Moreover, it seems likely that Tertullian views the *Agape* as the Lord's Supper itself since he contrasts its practice with the meals held by the pagans in honor of Hercules and Serapis. It would be strange if the parallel he makes does not correspond to the Lord's Supper.

B. Clement of Alexandria

In his *The Instructor*, Clement of Alexandria writes extensively about the *Agape*. As with Tertullian above, we cannot know with certainty whether the Eucharist is to be included in Clement's *Agape*.

---

[38] Marshall, *Last Supper and Lord's Supper*, 111.

[39] Ibid. 145.

[40] Tertullian, *Apology* 39:16, *The Fathers of the Church: A New Translation*, vol. 10, ed. R. J. Defarrari, trans. R. Arbesmann, et al. (Washington, DC.: Catholic University of America Press, 1950), 101.

However, there are indications that Clement sees the *Agape* and the Eucharist as integral parts of the same practice. When contrasting the Christian *Agape* with the feasts practiced by non-Christians he writes: "But we who seek the heavenly bread must rule the belly."[41] This can only be an allusion to John 6.

Clement's language sometimes suggests that he is against the idea of a Christian feast altogether; yet it is clear that Clement is interested only in the separation of extravagance from the meal, not in abandoning the meal itself.[42] He believes the *Agape* should be a means of showing love to the poor,[43] and is meant to provide sustenance, not pleasure.[44] Far from abandoning the *Agape*, Clement desires only to correct potential abuses of it.

C. The Letter of Pliny

One of the earliest pieces of evidence that we have for the post-apostolic practice of the early church is that found in a letter of Pliny to the Emperor Trajan dated about AD 111-112. In this letter Pliny relates the testimony of former Christians who have defected and renounced Christ. The portion of the letter that alludes to the *Agape* is one that is often cited in quips and quotes in some of the more popular manuals of church history:

> They were in the habit of meeting on a certain fixed day before sunrise and reciting an antiphonal hymn to Christ as God, and binding themselves with an oath—not to commit any crime, but to abstain from all acts of theft, robbery and adultery, from breaches of faith, from denying a trust when called upon to honor it. After this, they went on, it was their custom to separate, and then to meet again to partake of food, but food of an ordinary and innocent kind. And even this, they said, they had given up doing since the publication of my edict in which, according to your instructions, I had placed a ban on private associations.[45]

---

[41] Clement of Alexandria, *The Instructor*, Book 2, 1:1, in *Ante-Nicene Fathers*, vol. 2, ed. A. Roberts and J. Donaldson (Peabody, MA: Hendrickson Publishing, 1994), 238.

[42] Ibid., v. 15.

[43] Ibid., vv. 7, 11.

[44] Ibid., v. 8.

[45] *Pliny to the Emperor Trajan* 96, Book 10, vol. 2, rev. W. M. L. Hutchinson, trans. W.

The last two sentences are of particular interest to those attempting to pinpoint the exact date of the cessation of the *Agape*. Clearly Pliny can be describing nothing other than the Christian feast, and for this reason many scholars have seen in this edict the end of the *Agape* as practiced in the first century. Wainwright echoes the widely accepted view that the phrase, "even this they had given up doing since my edict," refers to the church at large abandoning the common meal.[46] Goguel sees the word *sacramentum* ("oath") as evidence that the Eucharist was transferred to the morning meeting after Pliny's edict against social gatherings.[47] Kasper sees this as "clear evidence" for the separation of the Eucharist from the *Agape* in the second century.[48]

But just how this letter supports the separation of the Eucharist from the *Agape* is not so apparent. Against Goguel's view, *sacramentum* is probably best taken here as "oath."[49] Moreover, Pliny speaks of the *sacramentum* as being practiced in the morning during the same pre-edict period as when the common meal was practiced in the evening. What reason then would there be for separating meal from Eucharist if they were being practiced separately *before* the edict?

The strongest argument for the cessation of the *Agape* in Pliny is the statement to which Wainwright refers:

> It was their custom to separate, and then to meet again to partake of food, but food of an ordinary and innocent kind. And even this, they said, they had given up doing since the publication of my edict in which, according to your instructions, I had placed a ban on private associations.

Wainwright (among others) takes this to mean that the church universally abandoned the meal aspect due to the edict of Pliny that banned private associations. This assumes however that "they" refers

---

Melmoth (Cambridge: Harvard University Press, 1961), 403-405.

[46] Wainwright, 76.

[47] M. Goguel, *The Primitive Church*, trans. H. C. Snape (New York: Macmillan, 1964), 359.

[48] Kasper, 132.

[49] With Bruce, *New Testament History*, 424. Cf. *The Oxford Latin Dictionary* (ed. P. G. W. Glare [Oxford: Clarendon Press, 1983]) which gives the meaning, "an oath made to an organization," military or otherwise; and *The Latin-English Lexicon* (ed. E. A. Andrews [New York: Harper & Brothers Publications, 1852]), which gives the meanings "a military oath of allegiance, a [non- military] oath, a solemn obligation."

to the entire church. It is more likely, in view of the fact that this is a report from ex-Christians who were making statements in denial of the charge that they were continuing in their associations with other Christians, that "they" refers here not to the church, but to these ex-Christians only. In other words, the ex-Christians had given up meeting with the church since the publication of the edict. These may have been nominal Christians who had joined the ranks of the church perhaps for social reasons and left for purposes of expediency; namely, the threat of execution![50] Moreover, it is doubtful that the phrase, "and even this, they said, they had given up doing since the publication of my edict," pertains to the *Agape* specifically, but more likely refers to any meeting with the church. Indeed, the ban was placed upon "private associations," not specifically cultic meals. It was the apostate Christians who had "given up" meeting together, not the church.

D. The *Didache*

One other significant writing of the early second century that deserves mention in regard to the *Agape* is the *Didache*. In *Did.* 14 there are instructions on gathering together, one reason of which is to break bread. *Didache* 9-10, however, gives more explicit details about the early second-century procedure for the eucharistic celebration. In *Did.* 10, immediately after the instructions about the sayings over the bread and cup, the writer says: "And after you are *satisfied*, thus give thanks,"[51] and then proceeds to give instructions about prayer after the meal. The writer implies a meal here, for who could become "satisfied" on token elements? He makes the same allusion to a meal in the prayer said after the meal: "You, Almighty Master, created all things for your name's sake, and gave food and drink to men for *enjoyment*."[52] The food for which the writer gives thanks is for "enjoyment," not for representation. The allusion to a meal in connection with the Eucharist is revealing, for it indicates that the *Agape* was still

---

[50] The punishment for persistent refusal to recant [Christianity] was death: "So far this has been my procedure when people were charged before me with being Christians. . . I ordered them to be led off to execution," *Pliny to Trajan*, Hutchinson, 401.

[51] Lightfoot and Harmer, 232.

[52] Ibid., 233.

very much a part of the Eucharist in the early second century.[53] It cannot be until later that the *Agape* faded from the scene. This in turn implies that there probably was no apostolic intent of the *Agape* ever ceasing. On the contrary, from Paul to Jude to the second-century church we have a consistent witness of a universal practice of the *Agape* without the slightest hint that it should not be practiced.

In the third and final part of this article, we will conclude our consideration of the Table of the Lord.

---

[53] Contra G. D. Kilpatrick (*The Eucharist in Bible and Liturgy*, Moorehouse Lectures 1975 [Cambridge: CUP, 1983], 20) who believes these texts not to be referring to the Eucharist but to "an ordinary Christian meal." Goguel (342), pointing out the similarities between chapters 9, 10, and 14, concludes that they all refer to the same rite.

SUBJECT INDEX OF THE *JOURNAL OF THE GRACE EVANGELICAL SOCIETY* (1988-2020)

JOHN YANTIS

I. EDITOR'S NOTE

These indexes of the *JOTGES* will be published in this and the spring journal. There is a subject index and a contributing authors index. In addition, there will be a listing of the editorial staff since the founding of the *Journal* as well as an issue cross reference. GES plans on putting these indexes online while keeping them up to date.

II. SUBJECT INDEX

Antichrist

"The Spirit of the Antichrist: Decoupling Jesus from the Christ," by Zane C. Hodges. Autumn 2007, 37-46.

Apologetics

We Believe: "Jesus Is Lord," by Arthur L. Farstad. Spring 1989, 3-11.

"Jewish Genius and the Existence of God," by Shawn C. Lazar. Spring 2016, 19-39.

"When Was Adam Created?" by Terry Mortenson. Spring 2017, 49-75.

Art

Grace in the Arts: "Rembrandt Van Ryn: A Protestant Artist," by Arthur L. Farstad. Spring 1993, 59-68.

Assurance

"Assurance: Of the Essence of Saving Faith," by Zane C. Hodges. Spring 1997, 3-17.

"Assurance and Works: An Evangelical Train Wreck," by Zane C. Hodges. Spring 2009, 31-35.

A Voice from the Past: "Assurance and Doubt," by John Calvin. Autumn 1990, 47-51.

We Believe In: "Assurance of Salvation," by Zane C. Hodges. Autumn 1990, 3-17; Spring 2009, 13-30.

"Does Anyone Really Know If They Are Saved? A Survey of the Current Views on Assurance With a Modest Proposal," by Ken Keathley. Spring 2002, 37-59.

"Full Assurance," by L.E. Brown. Autumn 2008, 29-41.

"Gordon H. Clark and Assurance," by Shawn C. Lazar. Autumn 2016, 35-48.

"The Practical Syllogism and Assurance," by Robert N. Wilkin. Autumn 2018, 19-34.

"A Review of Christopher D. Bass's *That You May Know: Assurance of Salvation in 1 John*," by Robert N. Wilkin. Autumn 2011, 3-22.

"A Review of Matthew C. Hoskinson's *Assurance of Salvation: Implications of a New Testament Theology of Hope*," by Robert N. Wilkin. Autumn 2019, 19-33.

A Voice from the Past: "Life Received," by James H. Brookes. Autumn 1999, 53-59.

"Romans 8:16 and Assurance," by Ken Yates. Autumn 2017, 3-17.

"Testing Yourself Regarding God's Approval and Disapproval (2 Corinthians 13:5-7)," by Robert N. Wilkin. Spring 2020, 21-39.

"When Assurance Is Not Assurance," by Robert N. Wilkin. Autumn 1997, 27-34.

Atonement

"Benefits of Christ's Blood: Restricted and Unrestricted," by Robert N. Wilkin. Autumn 2009, 3-10.

"Christ died for All: Unlimited Atonement According to Robert D. Preus and Zane C. Hodges," by Shawn C. Lazar. Autumn 2014, 45-60.

"Worthy to Reign: The Cross and the War for Dominion," by Shawn C. Lazar. Autumn 2017, 81-97.

Baptism

"The Gospel and Water Baptism: A Study of Acts 2:38," by Lanny Thomas Tanton. Spring 1990, 27-52.

"The Gospel and Water Baptism: Another Look at Acts 2:38," by Lanny Thomas Tanton. Autumn 2012, 55-89.

"The Gospel and Water Baptism: A Study of Acts 22:16," by Lanny Thomas Tanton. Spring 1991, 23-40.

"Is Our Understanding of Baptism All Wet?" by Brad Doskocil. Autumn 2015, 55-70.

We Believe In: "Water Baptism," by Arthur L. Farstad. Spring 1990, 3-9.

Bible

"Dating the New Testament," by Frank Tyler. Spring 2015, 37-50.

"A Free Grace Perspective on Bible Translations," by Robert N. Wilkin. Spring 2004, 3-14.

"Greek as the Spoken Language of Christ," by Jim Hitt. Spring 2018, 47-62.

"The New Revised Standard Version: A Review," by Arthur L. Farstad. Autumn 1990, 33-45.

"Pray that God's Word May Run and Be Glorified: 2 Thessalonians 3:1-2," by Robert N. Wilkin. Autumn 2013, 33-45.

"Review of Craig L. Blomberg's The Historical Reliability of John's Gospel: Issues & Commentary," by Edwin Ediger. Spring 2019, 83-101.

A Voice from the Past: "Priest or Prophet?" by W. H. Griffith Thomas. Spring 1996, 59-67.

"What Difference Does It Make? The Greek Text We Accept Makes a Big Difference," by Wilbur N. Pickering. Spring 2012, 37-65.

Calvinism

"Calvinism Ex Cathedra: A Review of John H. Gerstner's *Wrongly Dividing the Word of Truth: A Critique of Dispensationalism*," by Zane C. Hodges. Autumn 1991, 59-70.

"A Critique of *The Potter's Freedom* by James White," by Laurence M. Vance. Spring 2003, 29-34.

"Dortian Calvinism Is Dead Wrong on Ephesians 1: A Review of Timothy R. Nichols's *Dead Man's Faith*," by John H. Niemelä. Autumn 2019, 71-79.

"Ethical Inconsistencies in Calvinist Pastoral Ministry," by Allen M. Rea. Spring 2018, 63-78.

"The New Puritanism—Part 1: Carson on Christian Assurance," by Zane C. Hodges. Spring 1993, 19-31; Spring 2009, 37-51.

"The New Puritanism—Part 2: Michael S. Horton: Holy War with Unholy Weapons," by Zane C. Hodges. Autumn 1993, 25-38; Spring 2009, 53-66.

"The New Puritanism—Part 3: Michael S. Horton: Holy War with Unholy Weapons," by Zane C. Hodges. Spring 1994, 17-29; Spring 2009, 67-79.

"Racism, Southern Seminary, and the Perseverance of the Saints," by Ken Yates. Autumn 2019, 3-18.

"A Review of Dave Hunt's *What Love Is This? Calvinism's Misrepresentation of God*," by Laurence M. Vance. Autumn 2002, 41-44.

"A Review of R.C. Sproul's *Grace Unknown: The Heart of Reformed Theology*," by Robert N. Wilkin. Autumn 2001, 3-19.

"Soteriological Implications of Five-Point Calvinism," by Phillip F. Congdon. Autumn 1995, 55-68.

The Sovereignty of God: Contemporary Evangelical Attestation versus Biblical Attestation," by Jeremy D. Edmondson. Autumn 2018, 41-56.

"TULIP: A Free Grace Perspective Part 1: Total Depravity," by Anthony B. Badger. Spring 2003, 35-61.

"TULIP: A Free Grace Perspective Part 2: Unconditional Election," by Anthony B. Badger. Autumn 2003, 17-42.

"TULIP: A Free Grace Perspective Part 3: Limited Atonement," by Anthony B. Badger. Spring 2004, 33-56.

"TULIP: A Free Grace Perspective Part 4: Irresistible Grace," by Anthony B. Badger. Autumn 2004, 19-40.

"TULIP: A Free Grace Perspective Part 5: Perseverance of the Saints," by Anthony B. Badger. Autumn 2005, 15-42.

Christian Fiction

"The Billiard Parlor Evangel," by J. O. Hosler. Autumn 1988, 59-69.

Grace in the Arts: "The Alpha Strategem, Part 1," by Frank D. Carmical. Autumn 1994, 49-68.

Grace in the Arts: "The Alpha Strategem, Part 2," by Frank D. Carmical. Spring 1995, 55-72.

Grace in the Arts: "The Coronation of the King—Part 1," by Frank D. Carmical. Autumn 1989, 53-68.

Grace in the Arts: "The Coronation of the King—Part 2," by Frank D. Carmical. Spring 1990, 55-70.

Church

"Another Tale of Two Cities," by David R. Anderson. Autumn 2005, 51-76.

We Believe In: "The Church," by Arthur L. Farstad. Spring 1992, 3-10.

"Crossing the Tiber: What's Driving the Evangelical Exodus to Rome?" by Philippe R. Sterling. Spring 2020, 41-57.

"Evidence for a First Century 'Tenement Church'," by John Niemelä. Spring 2011, 99-116.

"Missional Ecclesiology in the Book of Acts," by L.E. Brown. Autumn 2011, 65-88.

"Seeker Friendly Churches and the Problem of Unregenerate Congregations," by Jeremy D. Edmondson. Spring 2013, 63-76.

"The Wisdom of God in Assembling," by Earl D. Radmacher. Autumn 2013, 9-31.

Confession

"Why Confess Christ? The Use and Abuse of Romans 10:9-10," by John Hart. Autumn 1999, 3-35.

"Confession of Sins in the Spirit-Filled Life," by Bob Bryant. Autumn 2001, 53-62.

Consensus theology

"Consensus Theology Taints Biblical Theology," by Stephen R. Lewis. Autumn 2010, 27-41.

Contemplative Spirituality and theology

"Christian Leadership and Mentoring: Contemplative Theology's Trojan Horse," by Philippe R. Sterling. Autumn 2007, 17-35.

"An Evaluation of Thomas à Kempis' *The Imitation of Christ*," by Lorne Zelyck. Autumn 2005, 77-88.

"A Review of Richard J. Foster's *Celebration of Discipline: The Path to Spiritual Growth*, Part 1," by Brad Doskocil. Spring 2019, 43-59.

"A Review of Richard J. Foster's *Celebration of Discipline: The Path to Spiritual Growth*, Part 2," by Brad Doskocil. Autumn 2019, 35-50.

"What is Contemplative Spirituality and Why Is It Dangerous? A Review of Brennan Manning's *The Signature of Jesus*," by John Caddock. Autumn 1997, 3-25.

Discipleship

"Acting on Our Union with Christ: Romans 6:12-23," by Zane C. Hodges. Autumn 2009, 11-18.

"Affluence Without Influence: The Laodicean Church in Revelation 3:14-22," by Joseph Lombardi. Autumn 2013, 97-112.

"Coming to Terms with Discipleship," by Charles C. Bing. Spring 1992, 35-49.

"A Critique of Bonhoeffer Speaks Today: Following Jesus at All Costs," by Samuel C. Smith. Autumn 2007, 71-78.

"The Cost of Discipleship," by Charles C. Bing. Spring 1993, 33-52.

"Discipleship and the Widow's Mites (Mark 12:41-44)," by Ken Yates. Spring 2020, 3-20.

"Free at Last! Freedom in Jesus' Footsteps (John 8:30-32)," by John Niemelä. Autumn 2018, 57-72.

"The Healing of Bartimaeus (Mark 10:46-52), Part 1," by Ken Yates. Spring 2016, 3-18.

"The Healing of Bartimaeus (Mark 10:46-52), Part 2," by Ken Yates. Autumn 2016, 3-15.

"Hebrews Provides a Model for How to Encourage 'Stuck' Believers to Get Growing," by David Janssen. Spring 2010, 75-92.

"How Deep Are Your Spiritual Roots? (Luke 8:11-15)," by Robert N. Wilkin. Spring 1999, 3-19.

"The Making of a Disciple," by Charles C. Bing. Autumn 1992, 27-43.

"A Review of John MacArthur's Hard to Believe: The High Cost and Infinite Value of Following Jesus," by Robert N. Wilkin. Autumn 2004, 3-9.

"The Secret Believer in the Gospel of John," by Bob Bryant. Autumn 2014, 61-75.

A Voice from the Past: "That I May Gain Christ: Philippians 3," by John Nelson Darby. Spring 2000, 37-42.

"Viticulture and John 15:1-6," by Gary W. Derickson. Spring 2005, 23-43.

Discipline

"'But If It Yields Thorns and Thistles:' An Exposition of Hebrews 5:11—6:12," by J. Paul. Tanner. Spring 2001, 19-42.

"Do Believers Experience the Wrath of God?" by René A Lopez. Autumn 2002, 45-66.

A Voice from the Past: "Simon Magus," by James Inglis. Spring 1989, 45-54.

Dispensationalism

"Does Christ Occupy David's Throne Now?" by Frederic R. Howe. Spring 2006, 65-70.

"Dispensationalism and Free Grace: Intimately Linked," by Grant Hawley. Spring 2011, 63-81.

"Dispensationalism and Free Grace: Intimately Linked, Part 2," by Grant Hawley. Autumn 2011, 89-106.

"Dispensationalism and Free Grace: Intimately Linked, Part 3," by Grant Hawley. Spring 2012, 21-36.

"Dispensationalism's Refusal of the Social Gospel and the Effect of Its Refusal on the Urgency of Evangelization," by Yoonhee Oh. Spring 2020, 79-98.

Ecumenism

"A Critique of Keith A. Fournier's *A House United? Evangelicals and Catholics Together: A Winning Alliance for the 21st Century*," by Robert N. Wilkin. Spring 1995, 11-29.

"A Dangerous Book or a Faulty Review? A Rejoinder to Robert Wilkin's Critique of *A House United?*" by William D. Watkins. Autumn 1995, 3-23.

"A Surrejoinder to William D. Watkins's Rejoinder to My Critique of *A House United?*" by Robert N. Wilkin. Autumn 1995, 25-37.

"*How Wide the Divide? A Mormon and an Evangelical in Conversation*: A Review," by Philip F. Congdon. Autumn, 2000, 67-72

Election

"The Doctrine of Divine Election Reconsidered: Election to Service, Not to Everlasting Life," by Robert N. Wilkin. Autumn 2012, 3-22.

"Making Your Call and Election Sure: 2 Peter 1:5-11," by Zane C. Hodges. Spring 1998, 21-33.

Eschatology

"Acts 1:8 Reconsidered: A Stub Track, A Siding, or a Main Track?" by John Niemelä. Autumn 2011, 49-63.

"The Two Modes of Humanity, Part 1: The View Delineated and Supported," by Philippe R. Sterling. Spring 2013, 49-62.

"The Two Modes of Humanity, Part 2: The History of the View," by Philippe R. Sterling. Spring 2014, 33-56.

"The Two Modes of Humanity, Part 3: Objections and Responses," by Philippe R. Sterling. Autumn 2014, 33-43.

"The Transfiguration of Christ," by S. Lewis Johnson. Spring 2015, 51-61.

Evangelism

"Another Look at the Deserted Island Illustration," by Robert N. Wilkin. Spring 2013, 3-20.

"A Critical Perspective: Orthodoxy, the Right Jesus, and Eternal Life," by Lon Gregg. Autumn 2009, 93-107.

"The Evangelistic Message of the Emerging Church," by Robert Vacendak. Autumn 2009, 55-73.

"God Uses Gospel Tracts," by Perry C. Brown. Autumn 1994, 25-36.

"How to Lead People to Christ, Part 1: The Content of Our Message," by Zane C. Hodges. Autumn 2000, 3-12; Spring 2009, 129-140.

"How to Lead People to Christ, Part 2: Our Invitation to Respond," by Zane C. Hodges. Spring 2001, 9-18; Spring 2009, 141-151.

"Is Ignorance Eternal Bliss?" by Robert N. Wilkin. Spring 2003, 3-15.

"Is There a Hole in Our Gospel? Does the Church Have a Social Commission Too?" by Philippe R. Sterling. Spring 2011, 83-97.

"'Jesus for You' – Gerhard Forde on Proclaiming the Promises of God," by Shawn C. Lazar. Autumn 2015, 41-53.

John 4:10: A Promise to the Samaritan Woman," by Frank W. Tyler. Autumn 2019, 51-69.

"Our Evangelism Should Be Exegetically Sound," by Robert N. Wilkin. Autumn 2014, 17-32.

"The Promise of Everlasting Life in Paul's First Recorded Sermon," by Zane C. Hodges. Autumn 2016, 63-76.

"A Response to Hodges: How to Lead a Person to Christ, Parts 1 and 2," by Gregory P. Sapaugh. Autumn 2001, 21-29.

"A Review of J.B.Hixson's Getting the Gospel Wrong: The Evangelical Crisis No One Is Talking About," by Robert N. Wilkin. Spring 2008, 3-28.

"The Soteriology of Charles Haddon Spurgeon and How It Impacted His Evangelism," by Jerry Harmon. Spring 2006, 43-63.

"The Use and Abuse of John 3:16: A Review of Max Lucado's Book, *3:16—The Numbers of Hope*," by Robert Vacendak. Spring 2008, 77-91.

"The Whirlpool's Deadly Trap: Disenfranchising Jesus," by Zane C. Hodges. Spring 2019, 61-68.

Faith

"All Faith is Good? (Titus 2:10)," by Ken Yates. Spring 2017, 3-16.

"Beware of Confusion about Faith," by Robert N. Wilkin. Spring 2005, 3-13.

"The Biblical View of Truth," by John W. Robbins. Spring 2005, 49-69.

"Faith Alive," by Sean Gerety. Autumn 2017, 71-80.

Giving

Gospel

"Does Free Grace Theology Diminish the Gospel? A Review of Wayne Grudem's *'Free Grace' Theology: 5 Ways It Diminishes the Gospel,* Part 3," by Robert N. Wilkin. Autumn 2017, 19-34.

"The Gospel is More Than 'Faith Alone in Christ Alone'," by Jeremy D. Myers. Autumn 2006, 33-56.

"The Gospel Under Siege," by Jeremy D. Myers. Autumn 2003, 43-48.

"How to Share the Gospel Clearly," by Charles C. Bing. Spring 1994, 51-65.

"Introducing John's Gospel: In the Upper Room with Jesus the Christ, Part 1 of 2," by Zane C. Hodges. Spring 2008, 29-44.

"Introducing John's Gospel: Miraculous Signs and Literary Structure, Part 2 of 2," by Zane C. Hodges. Autumn 2008, 15-27.

"The Subtle Danger of an Imprecise Gospel," by Robert N. Wilkin. Spring 1997, 41-60.

A Voice from the Past: "The Heart of the Gospel," by Arthur T. Pierson. Autumn 1997, 35-47.

A Voice from the Past: "Discovering the Gospel," by Lance B. (Doc) Latham. Spring 1999, 67-72.

A Voice from the Past: "Paul's Gospel," by William R. Newell. Spring 1994, 45-50.

A Voice from the Past: "What Is the Gospel," by H.A. Ironside. Autumn 1990, 47-51.

Grace

"Cheap Grace or Cheap Law? Dietrich Bonhoeffer and Gerhard Forde on the Nature of Law and Gospel," by Shawn C. Lazar. Spring 2013, 21-35.

"Colonial America's Rejection of Free Grace Theology," by L.E. Brown. Spring 2007, 39-63.

"A Review of Thomas Stegall's *The Gospel of the Christ*," by Robert N. Wilkin. Spring 2010, 3-29.

A Voice from the Past: "The Fundamentals of Grace," by Lewis Sperry Chafer. Autumn 1994, 37-48.

A Voice from the Past: "Grace," by D. L. Moody. Spring 1995, 45-53.

A Voice from the Past: "Grace Reigns," by Sir Robert Anderson. Autumn 1996, 61-70.

A Voice from the Past: "Man Does Not Know Grace," by W. P. MacKay. Spring 1990, 53-54.

"The Marrow Controversy," by Michael D. Makidon. Autumn 2003, 65-77.

"The Novelty of Free Grace Theology, Part 1," by Ken Yates. Spring 2014, 3-15.

"The Novelty of Free Grace Theology, Part 2: The Dangers of Following the Commentary Traditions," by Ken Yates. Autumn 2014, 3-15.

"Review of A.B. Caneday's *Lest after preaching to others I become disqualified: Grace and Warning in Paul's gospel (1 Corinthians 9:23-27)*," by Robert N. Wilkin. Spring 2011, 3-20.

"Correction Regarding the View of Ardel B. Caneday Concerning 1 Corinthians 9:23-27," by Robert N. Wilkin. Autumn 2011, 107-110.

"'Sons of God' and the Road to Grace (Romans 8:12-17)," by Ken Yates. Autumn 2006, 23-32.

A Voice from the Past: "The True Grace of God in Which You Stand," by J. N. Darby. Autumn 1995, 69-73.

Grace Evangelical Society

"An Introduction to Grace Evangelical Society and Its Journal," by Arthur L. Farstad. Autumn 1988, 3-10.

"Zane Hodges and GES Did Not Change the Gospel," by Don Reiher. Spring 2010, 31-58.

Hermeneutics

"'Abraham rejoiced to See My Day and Saw It': Jesus' Take on Theophanies," by Randy Rheaume. Spring 2019, 69-82.

"The Confession of the Centurion in Luke 23:47," by Ken Yates. Spring 2019, 3-22.

"I Mean Both: Double Meanings in John's Gospel," by Gary W. Derickson. Spring 2018, 79-93.

"Jesus' Intervention in the Temple: Once or Twice?" by Allan Chapple. Autumn 2020, 67-99.

"Jesus' Use of Spittle in Mark 8:22-26," by Ken Yates. Spring 2015, 3-15.

"The Pentecostal Response (Acts 2:27-47)," by H.A. Ironside. Autumn 2015, 37-39.

"Rethinking the New Testament Concept of Perishing," by Robert N. Wilkin. Autumn 2010, 3-26.

"Revelation 3:10 and the Rapture: A New Departure," by John Niemelä. Spring 2017, 35-47.

"Review of Allan Chapple's 'Jesus' Intervention in the Temple: Once or Twice?'," by Robert N. Wilkin. Spring 2016, 91-96.

"A Review of Peter M. Phillips's *The Prologue of the Fourth Gospel*," by Bob Swift. Autumn 2009, 45-54.

"Sacrifice No Longer Remains: Hebrews 10:26-27," by John Niemelä. Autumn 2013, 65-77.

"So You May Come (or Continue?) to Believe (John 20:31," by John Niemelä. Spring 2016, 73-89.

"The Stone/Rock/Tomb Motif in Matthew," by Bob Swift. Autumn 2018, 35-40.

"That I May Attain to Whose Resurrection? Philippians 3:11," by John Niemelä. Autumn 2012, 23-35.

Inerrancy

"Repopulating After the Flood: Was Cainan or Shelah the Son of Arphaxad?" by Wilbur N. Pickering. Spring 2005, 45-48.

"Toward a Narrow View of *Ipsissima Vox*," by Bob Wilkin. Spring 2001, 3-8.

Judgment

"Believers and the Bema," by Earl D. Radmacher. Spring 1995, 31-43.

"'The Day' is the Judgment Seat of Christ," by Robert N. Wilkin. Autumn 2007, 3-15.

"For Whom Does Hebrews 10:26-31 Teach a 'Punishment Worse Than Death?'" by J. Paul Tanner. Autumn 2006, 57-77.

"Keep Yourselves in the Love of God – A Study of Jude 20-23," by Shawn Leach. Spring 2011, 47-61.

"Two Judgments and Four Types of People (Luke 19:11-27)," by Robert N. Wilkin. Spring 2012, 3-20.

"When Is the Judgment Seat of Christ?" by John Claeys. Spring 2018, 35-45.

"Will the Bad Deeds of Believers Be Considered at the Judgment Seat of Christ?" by Robert N. Wilkin. Spring 2015, 17-36.

Justification

"The British Antinomian Controversies," by Jonathan W. Arnold. Autumn 2012, 55-89.

"Evangelical/Roman Catholic Agreement on the Doctrine of Justification and its Ramifications for Grace Theologians," by Philip F. Congdon. Spring 2000, 11-23.

"God's Righteousness Has Been Revealed to Men: Romans 3:21-31," by Zane C. Hodges. Autumn 2010, 77-92.

"John Piper's Diminished Doctrine of Justification and Assurance," by Philip F. Congdon. Spring 2010, 59-73.

"Justification: A New Covenant Blessing," by Zane C. Hodges. Autumn 2006, 79-85; Spring 2009, 99-105.

"Justification and Judgment," by John W. Robbins. Spring 2002, 61-74.

"Is Justification by Faith Alone?" by Robert N. Wilkin. Autumn 1996, 3-20.

"Is Justification by Faith Part of The Gospel?" by Robert N. Wilkin. Autumn 2005, 3-14.

"A Response to Robert Sungenis's *Not by Faith Alone*," by Robert N. Wilkin. Autumn 2003, 3-16.

Legalism

"Legalism: The Real Thing," by Zane C. Hodges. Autumn 1996, 21-32; Spring 2009, 107-119.

"Review of Bryan Fraser's Winning a Generation Without the Law," by L.E. Brown. Spring 2011, 21-46.

Literature

Grace in the Arts: "Annie Dillard: Mistaken Mystic?" by James A. Townsend. Spring 2007, 65-78.

Grace in the Arts: "The Bronte Sisters: A Ministerial Home Without Much *Blessed Assurance*," by James A. Townsend. Autumn 2001, 63-92.

Grace in the Arts: "C. S. Lewis's Theology: Somewhere between Ransom and Reepicheep," by James A. Townsend. Spring 2000, 43-73.

Grace in the Arts: "Charles Dickens: Cheshire Cat 'Christianity'," by James A. Townsend. Autumn 1999, 61-82.

"*The Da Vinci Code* Phenomenon: A Brief Overview and Response," by J.B. Hixson. Autumn 2004, 41-48.

Grace in the Arts: "Dostoevsky and His Theology," by James Townsend. Autumn 1997, 49-68.

Grace in the Arts: "F.W. Boreham: Essayist Extraordinaire," by James A. Townsend. Spring 2001, 57-77.

Grace in the Arts: "G.K. Chesterton: The Theology of Philip Yancey's Favorite Writer," by James A. Townsend. Autumn 2002, 67-91.

Grace in the Arts: "Grace Abounding—In Great Literature," by James Townsend. Autumn 1990, 53-64.

Grace in the Arts: "Herman Melville: An Author in the Angst of Ambiguity," by James A. Townsend. Spring 2004, 57-83.

Grace in the Arts: "Jesus and Emily: The Biblical Roots of Emily Dickinson's Poetry," by Arthur L. Farstad. Autumn 1991, 45-57.

Grace in the Arts: "The Limits of Graciousness," by James Townsend. Spring 1989, 55-66.

Grace in the Arts: "Mark Twain: A Bitter Battle with God," by James A. Townsend. Autumn 2004, 49-76.

Grace in the Arts: "Robert Louis Stevenson: So Near, Yet So Far," by James A. Townsend. Spring 1999, 73-101.

Grace in the Arts: "Shakespeare, the Bible, and Grace," by Arthur L. Farstad. Spring 1991, 47-63.

Grace in the Arts: "The Theology of Leo Tolstoy," by James Townsend. Spring 1998, 59-81.

Grace in the Arts: "Thomas Hardy: The Tragedy of a Life Without Christ," by James Townsend. Spring 1997, 69-82.

Lordship Salvation

"A Critique of *The Gospel According to Jesus*," by J. Kevin Butcher. Spring 1989, 27-43.

"Dangerous Words: A Review of *Crazy Love* by Francis Chan," by Bruce Bauer. Autumn 2009, 75-91.

"An Evaluation of Some Evidences For 'Lordship Salvation,'" by Paul Holloway. Autumn 1989, 23-34.

"The High Cost of Salvation by Faith-Works: A Critique of John F. MacArthur, Jr.'s *Faith Works: The Gospel According to the Apostles*," by Robert N. Wilkin. Autumn 1993, 3-24.

"The Moralistic Wrath-Dodger," by Zane C. Hodges. Spring 2005, 15-21; Spring 2009, 121-128.

"The Psychological Effects of Lordship Salvation," by Frank B. Minirth. Autumn 1993, 39-51.

"A Return to Rome: Lordship Salvation's Doctrine of Faith," by Paul Holloway. Autumn 1991, 13-21.

"Why Lordship Faith Misses the Mark for Discipleship," by Charlie Bing. Autumn 1999, 37-52.

"Why Lordship Faith Misses the Mark for Salvation," by Charlie Bing. Spring 1999, 21-35.

Lord's Supper

We Believe In: "The Lord's Supper," by Arthur L. Farstad. Spring 1991, 3-12.

Millennial Kingdom

"The Church: Chosen to Reign (Ephesians 1:4-5)," by Ken Yates. Autumn 2018, 3-18.

"Law and Grace in the Millennial Kingdom," by Zane C. Hodges. Spring 2007, 31-38.

"Making Sense of the Millennium: Resurrection in Revelation 20," by Doros Zachariades. Autumn 2001, 31-51.

"The 'Outer Darkness' in Matthew and Its Relationship to Grace," by Michael G. Huber. Autumn 1992, 11-25.

"A Response to J. Paul Tanner's 'The Outer Darkness in Matthew's Gospel'," by Robert N. Wilkin. Spring 2018, 19-34.

Music

Grace in the Arts: "An Evangelical Musical Genius: 'J.S.B.:S.D.G.,'" by Arthur L. Farstad. Spring 1996, 69-75.

Grace in the Arts: "Marian Anderson and the Heritage of Spirituals," by Arthur L. Farstad. Autumn 1993, 57-75.

A Hymn of Grace: "All Hail the Power," by Frances Mosher. Autumn 1994, 89-91.

A Hymn of Grace: "Amazing Grace," by Arthur L. Farstad. Autumn 1989, 101-103.

A Hymn of Grace: "'At Calvary': A Gospel Song of Grace," by Frances Mosher. Spring 1994, 89-91.

A Hymn of Grace: "Grace Greater Than Our Sin," by Frances Mosher. Autumn 1992, 95-96.

A Hymn of Grace: "I'm a Child of the King," by Frances Mosher. Spring 1999, 117-118.

A Hymn of Grace: "Jehovah Tsidkenu: The Lord Our Righteousness," by Arthur L. Farstad. Spring 1992, 97-99.

A Hymn of Grace: "Jesus Lives and So Shall I," by Frances Mosher. Spring 1993, 95-96.

A Hymn of Grace: "Jesus, Thy Blood and Righteousness," by Frances Mosher. Autumn 1996, 99-101.

A Hymn of Grace: "Lord, with Glowing Heart I'd Praise Thee," by Arthur L. Farstad and Frances A. Mosher. Spring 1995, 95-98.

A Hymn of Grace: "No Other Plea," by Frances Mosher. Autumn 1997, 85-87.

A Hymn of Grace: "Not What These Hands Have Done," by Frances Mosher. Autumn 1991, 93-94.

A Hymn of Grace: "Once For All," by Frances Mosher. Spring 1991, 99-100.

A Hymn of Grace: "The Passion of the Apostle John," by Bob Kenagy. Autumn 1999, 109-113.

A Hymn of Grace: "Psalm 51: A Psalm of Grace," by Arthur L. Farstad. Autumn 1990, 93-94.

A Hymn of Grace: "Rock of Ages," by Frances Mosher. Autumn 1995, 97-99.

A Hymn of Grace: "Seasons of Rapture," by Frances Mosher. Autumn 1998, 93-94.

A Hymn of Grace: "The Solid Rock," by Keith W. Ward. Spring 1998, 105-108.

A Hymn of Grace: "To God Be the Glory," by Keith W. Ward. Spring 1996, 97-99.

A Hymn of Grace: "Sweet Little Jesus Boy," by Frances Mosher. Autumn 1993, 91-92.

A Hymn of Grace: "Where Shall My Wond'ring Soul Begin?" by James A. Townsend. Spring 1990, 95-97.

A Hymn of Grace: "Wonderful Grace of Jesus," by Keith W. Ward. Spring 1997, 99-101.

"Taking a Fresh Look at Some Popular Hymns of the Faith," by Robert N. Wilkin. Spring 2000, 3-10.

Grace in the Arts: "Toward Singing with the Understanding: A Discussion of the Gospel Hymn—Part 1," by Frances Mosher. Spring 1992, 55-76.

Grace in the Arts: "Toward Singing with the Understanding: A Discussion of the Gospel Hymn—Part 2," by Frances Mosher. Autumn 1992, 57-65.

"Worship Wars: Theological Persepctives on Hymnody Among Early Evangelical Christians," by Steve Lemke. Spring 2014, 57-79.

Mysticism

"Does God Give Subjective Revelation Today? The Place of Mysticism in Christian Experience," by Ken Hornok. Spring 2007, 15-30.

Perseverance

A Voice from the Past: "The Perseverance of the Saints," by Frederick W. Grant. Spring 1993, 53-57.

"Does Philippians 1:6 Guarantee Progressive Sanctification? Part 1," by John F. Hart. Spring 1996, 37-58.

"Does Philippians 1:6 Guarantee Progressive Sanctification? Part 2," by John F. Hart. Autumn 1996, 33-60.

"Perseverance: It Ain't Over Till It's Over," by Stephen R. Lewis. Autumn 2009, 19-28.

"The Perseverance of the Saints? Identifying Augustine's Influence on Evangelical Views of Apostasy," by Everett Berry. Autumn 2016, 49-62.

Postmodernism

"The Gospel According to Evangelical Postmodernism," by Robert N. Wilkin. Spring 2007, 3-13

"Post-Evangelicalism Confronts the Postmodern Age: A Review of *The Challenge of Postmodernism*," by Zane C. Hodges. Spring 1996, 3-14.

"Postmodernism: The Death of God and the Rise of the Community," by Michael D. Makidon. Spring 2004, 15-31.

Propitiation

"The Message That Gives Life and the Doctrine of Propitiation," by Stephen R. Lewis. Autumn 2013, 79-95.

"What Do We Mean By Propitiation? Does It Only Count If We Accept It?" by Zane C. Hodges. Spring 2006, 35-42.

Rapture

"Should Pretribulationists Reconsider the Rapture in Matthew 24:36-44? Part 1," by John F. Hart. Autumn 2007, 47-70.

"Should Pretribulationists Reconsider the Rapture in Matthew 24:36-44? Part 2 of 3," by John F. Hart. Spring 2008, 45-63.

"Should Pretribulationists Reconsider the Rapture in Matthew 24:36-44? Part 3 of 3," by John F. Hart. Autumn 2008, 43-64.

Repentance

"A Cloudy View of Salvation: David W. Cloud on Repentance," by Shawn C. Lazar. Autumn 2018, 73-86.

"Does Your Mind Need Changing? Repentance Reconsidered," by Robert N. Wilkin. Spring 1998, 35-46.

"Is the Concept of Repentance Found in John's Gospel, and If So, What Difference Does It Make?" by Robert N. Wilkin. Spring 2019, 23-41.

"Repentance and Faith in Acts 20:21," by Ken Yates. Spring 2018, 3-18.

"Repentance and Salvation—Part 1: The Doctrine of Repentance in Church History," by Robert N. Wilkin. Autumn 1988, 11-20.

"Repentance and Salvation—Part 2: The Doctrine of Repentance in the Old Testament," by Robert N. Wilkin. Spring 1989, 13-26.

"Repentance and Salvation—Part 3: New Testament Repentance: Lexical Considerations," by Robert N. Wilkin. Autumn 1989, 13-21.

"Repentance and Salvation—Part 4: New Testament Repentance: Repentance in the Gospels and Acts," by Robert N. Wilkin. Spring 1990, 11-25.

"Repentance and Salvation—Part 5: The Doctrine of Repentance in the Epistles and Revelation," by Robert N. Wilkin. Autumn 1990, 19-32.

"Repentance and Salvation—Part 6: Preaching and Teaching about Repentance," by Robert N. Wilkin. Spring 1991, 13-22.

"Repentance Is for All Men," by David R. Anderson. Spring 1998, 3-20.

"The National Repentance of Israel," by David R. Anderson. Autumn 1998, 13-37.

Rewards

"The Biblical Distinction Between Eternal Salvation and Eternal Rewards: A Key to Proper Exegesis," by Robert N. Wilkin. Spring 1996, 15-24.

"A Call to the Wedding Celebration: An Exposition of Matthew 22:1-14," by Gregory P. Sapaugh. Spring 1992, 11-34.

"Christians Who Lose Their Legacy: Galatians 5:21," by Robert N. Wilkin. Autumn 1991, 23-37.

"Degrees of Rewards in Eternity: Sanctification by Works?" by Douglas C. Bozung. Autumn 2011, 23-47.

"Hebrews 12:14: A Test Case for the Run-for-the-Prize View," by John H. Niemelä. Autumn 2010, 43-60.

"Inheritance in Hebrews Requires Obedience," by René A. López. Autumn 2010, 61-75.

"Mission, Godliness, and Reward in 2 Peter 1:5-11," by L.E. Brown. Spring 2012, 67-93.

"Secure Yet Scrutinized—2 Timothy 2:11-13," by Brad McCoy. Autumn 1988, 21-33.

A Voice from the Past: "Sonship and Heirship," by C. H. Mackintosh. Spring 1997, 61-68.

We Believe In: "Rewards," by Zane C. Hodges. Autumn 1991, 3-11; Spring 2009, 81-90.

Salvation

"Belief as a Cognitive Phenomenon, Especially in Regard to Salvation: An Expanded Discussion," by Richard M. Biery. Spring 2016, 57-72.

"The Condition for Salvation in John's Gospel," by Charles C. Bing. Spring 1996, 25-36.

"An Exegetical Study of the Lord's Logion on the 'Salvation of the *Psychē*'," by Jerry Pattillo. Autumn 2015, 21-36.

"Dallas Theological Seminary on Salvation: A Survey of Some Popular Professors Between 1965-1990," by Shawn C. Lazar. Spring 2020, 59-78.

"How Were People Saved Before Jesus Came?" by Bob Bryant. Spring 2003, 63-70.

"Jacob's Eternal Salvation and Genesis 32," by Kathryn Wright. Autumn 2020, 35-54.

"Matthew 25:31-46: Salvation by Works," by John Claeys. Autumn 2017, 55-70.

"Old Testament Salvation – From What?" by René A. López. Autumn 2003, 49-64.

"Pre-Reformation Belief in Eternal Security: The Word of Faith We Preach Is Near (Romans 10:8)," by John H. Niemelä. Spring 2015, 63-80.

"A Review and Application of Albert Mohler's *We Cannot Be Silent*," by Kathryn Wright. Spring 2017, 77-89.

"Salvation and the Sovereignty of God: The Great Commission as the Expression of the Divine Will," by Ken Keathley. Spring 2006, 3-22.

"Salvation as Spiritual Health in 1 Corinthians," by Robert N. Wilkin. Autumn 2020, 19-34.

"'Salvation' in the Book of Philippians," by Robert C. Swift. Spring 2016, 41-56.

"The Salvation of Believing Israelites Prior to the Incarnation of Christ," by Sidney D. Dyer. Spring 2001, 43-55.

"The Soteriological Concerns with Bauer's Greek Lexicon," by Michael D. Makidon. Autumn 2004, 11-18.

"The Soteriological Impact of Augustine's Change from Premillennialism to Amillennialism: Part One," by David R. Anderson. Spring 2002, 25-36.

"The Soteriological Impact of Augustine's Change from Premillennialism to Amillennialism: Part Two," by David R. Anderson. Autumn 2002, 23-39.

"Striving for the Prize of Eternal Salvation: A Review of Schreiner and Caneday's The Race Set Before Us," by Robert N. Wilkin. Spring 2002, 3-24.

"Regeneration: A Crux Interpretum," by David R. Anderson. Autumn 2000, 43-65.

"Regeneration: A New Covenant Blessing," by Zane C. Hodges. Autumn 2005, 43-49; Spring 2009, 91-97.

"Universal Sin and Salvation in Romans 5:12-21," by Mark Rapinchuk. Autumn 2017, 35-54.

A Voice from the Past: "Assurance of Faith and Possession of Salvation," by César Malan. Autumn 1989, 35-52.

A Voice from the Past: "The Knowledge of Salvation," by George Cutting. Autumn 1991, 39-44.

A Voice from the Past: "Look and Live," by Robert Murray McCheyne. Spring 1992, 51-53.

A Voice from the Past: "Salvation by Grace," by J. Irvin Overholtzer. Autumn 1998, 53-62.

A Voice from the Past: "The Terms of Salvation," by Lewis Sperry Chafer. Autumn 1988, 35-57.

BOOK REVIEWS

Tethered to the Cross: The Life and Preaching of C. H. Spurgeon.
**By Thomas Breimaier. Downers Grove, IL: IVP Academic, 2020.
271 pp. Hardcover, $24.64.**

Thomas Breimaier is a professor at Spurgeon's College in London. In this work, he analyzes Spurgeon's approach to hermeneutics. C. H. Spurgeon (1834-1892) was perhaps the most famous preacher of his day, ministering in London. He viewed all of the Bible through the cross of Christ and sought the spiritual conversion of his hearers. His desire was that his preaching would also lead those that were already converted to have a deeper knowledge of the Bible and more effectively engage in evangelism (pp. 3-4).

Spurgeon was extraordinarily successful. He was the pastor of the Metropolitan Tabernacle and often preached to thousands. When he died, over fifty-six million copies of his sermons had been sold. He published a widely read magazine, *The Sword and the Trowel,* and ran a pastor's college to train men to follow in his model of ministry. In addition, he established two orphanages and reached out to the poor of his day to meet their physical needs. He would also on occasion comment on political and social ills (pp. 119-21, 182).

There are chapters which address Spurgeon's theological education, his early and later years, and how he trained the pastors in his college. Chapters 3 and 4, which deal with how Spurgeon used both the Old and New Testaments to point people to the cross, will probably be of most interest to the readers of the *JOTGES.*

Spurgeon credits a sermon on Isa 45:22 as leading to his own conversion at the age of 15, when he heard a preacher in a Methodist church expound on it. Even though the death of Christ is not found in the passage, the preacher said that it pointed to the cross. This would later provide the pattern of Spurgeon's ministry, when he would take a single verse and concentrate on the crucifixion of the Lord (p. 23). The immediate context was not important (p. 79). He would preach out of all types of OT literature and point his hearers to Christ's substitutionary atonement (pp. 105, 109). Breimaier says

Spurgeon often engaged in "creative" interpretation in both the OT and NT (p. 168). As a result, Spurgeon rejected Biblical interpretation based upon a "plain, literal, sense" (p. 234).

Spurgeon did not obtain a formal theological education but was a voracious reader. He commented that a woman who was a cook taught him as a young believer more than a theological education could have. Interestingly, she was known as an antinomian, and he credits her with removing many "doubts" in his mind (p. 30). Breimaier does not mention in the book if this is when Spurgeon gained assurance of his eternal salvation, or if he ever did. In the book, the closest Spurgeon comes to a Free Grace gospel was when he asked a sinner if he would believe. The person was to believe that Christ died on the cross so that he might not die (p. 120).

It is difficult to determine exactly what Spurgeon thought the gospel of eternal life involved. Breimaier offers numerous quotes from Spurgeon, but none mention assurance, and eternal life or its equivalent is rarely mentioned. Faith for Spurgeon seems to mean looking at the death of Christ on the cross (p. 35). Spurgeon emphasized the suffering and death of Jesus and how the unbeliever would be convicted of sin as the result of the price Christ paid. On the cross, the Lord paid for the sins of the unbeliever (p. 99). The unsaved needed to hate their sin (p. 145).

Spurgeon seemed to have an eclectic theology. He claimed to have a vision of hell on one occasion, which led him to a particularly powerful sermon (p. 40). He drew inspiration from Puritans, Methodists, Anglicans, and Baptists (p. 42). He disagreed with strict Calvinists in that he said that Christ died for the whole world and that people have free will to be converted (pp. 52-53). Spurgeon was a strong believer in the inerrancy of Scriptures and was a critic of higher criticism (pp. 85-89). He would plead for sinners to "wholly" and "really" trust in Christ as their Redeemer (p. 112).

It will be of interest to the readers of the *JOTGES* that Spurgeon was a strong opponent of Dispensationalism and thought that trying to understand eschatology was mostly a waste of time (pp. 139, 161). He would also be comfortable with a Lordship Salvation understanding of the gospel. A person who claims he has repented of sin must prove it by his life. If he claims to be a Christian but does not have a sufficient amount of good works, he is a liar (p. 149).

There were controversies in the ministry of Spurgeon. In addition to his disagreements with Calvinists in some areas, the Downgrade Controversy (1887-88) put him in conflict with the Baptists of his day over the issues of the inspiration of the Scriptures, liberal views of the atonement, and the eternality of hell (pp. 93, 195). He would resign from the Baptist Union over the controversy and find himself aligned with many in the Church of England that agreed with him in these areas (p. 195), even though he previously had accused them of hypocrisy and disagreed with them in other areas, such as infant baptism. He would even use them as professors in his pastors' college (p. 210). He could minister with those who pointed people to the cross and sought the conversion of sinners, regardless of other differences.

Charles Spurgeon died at the age of 57 after years of poor health. His physical difficulties did not prevent him from working hard in his various ministries. He became one of the most famous preachers in the history of Christendom. His life makes an excellent study. Breimaier has done an outstanding job of explaining what formed the basis of Spurgeon's preaching. He pointed people to the cross and wanted them to be aware of the price for their sins that Jesus paid. Those who did the same were his partners in ministry. The issues of assurance or eternal security, as well as the role of works in spiritual salvation, were not paramount. Spurgeon could work with Arminians, Calvinists, and even those in the Church of England. While he was an avid reader and strong student of theology, his hermeneutic principles did not require that he exegete any passage on which he spoke. The cross of Christ was to be elevated, whether that passage spoke of it or not.

It cannot be denied that in his day Spurgeon was extremely popular and his writings and sermons have been studied ever since. However, it is fair to ask if his view of the gospel was Biblical and if his hermeneutics should be followed by students of the Bible today. I highly recommend this book.

Kenneth W. Yates
Editor
Journal of the Grace Evangelical Society

***Without a Doubt: How to Know for Certain That You're Good with God.* By Dean Inserra. Chicago, IL: Moody Publishers, 2020. 79 pp. Paper, $7.99.**

Great title.

Great subtitle.

But then I read the book.

There are some Calvinists like David Engelsma who believe in the certainty of everlasting life. Calvinists like Engelsma base assurance solely on the promise of everlasting life that the Lord Jesus makes to all who believe in Him. However, most Calvinists, including Inserra, are on a lifelong quest for assurance. Engelsma calls the evangelistic message of such Calvinists "a gospel of doubt."

Inserra implies in the title and subtitle that it is possible to be certain of one's eternal destiny. In several places in this short book, Inserra says that believers can and should be sure. For example, the last sentence of the book reads, "Trust in Christ, repent of your sins, and never have to wonder where you stand with God again" (p. 75). As can be seen, Inserra does not mention believing the promise of life there. He mentions trusting in Christ and repenting of your sins. And he does not say that if you do those things you will be certain. He says if you do those things then you never need to wonder. In the rest of the book he explains what you need to do to avoid wondering where you stand.

The first difficulty, as seen in the quote just cited, is that Inserra believes that trusting in Christ (faith in Christ?) is not enough to be born again. You must also repent of your sins. Of course, that raises questions of subjectivity. I did not know all my sins in the past. Nor do I know all my sins in the present. If turning from my sins is a condition of the new birth, then I will always wonder if I have turned from enough of them.

The second difficulty is that Inserra says, quoting another author (Menikoff) favorably, "Though this belief is more than intellectual adherence to sound doctrine, it is not less" (p. 38). Inserra says that one must intellectually adhere to the facts that Jesus died for our sins, was buried, rose bodily from the dead, and appeared to many (1 Cor 15:3-11). He is not clear what other aspects of "sound doctrine" one must be convinced are true. But faith in Christ is "more than intellectual adherence" to the facts. A few pages later he indicated what more besides faith is required: "While believing in Jesus and His gospel are essential, He also included the call to repent, to turn from one's sin and follow Jesus and His teachings" (p. 42). How does one know if he is following Jesus and His teachings well enough?

Most Calvinists are not quite as clear as Inserra on degrees of assurance. He favorably quotes an author (Ferguson) who says, "high degrees of Christian assurance are simply not compatible with low levels of obedience" (p. 43). That is clever. But the point is disturbing. The more obedience one has, the higher his degree of assurance. The less obedience, the less assurance. The conclusion is unmistakable that the only way one could be sure is if he had perfect obedience. But wait. Even then, he could not be sure that he would not sin in the future.

The last chapter before the conclusion is entitled, "Marks of a Transformed Life" (p. 63). In this chapter Inserra says, "I believe it is important to give tangible examples of what a life lived by a saving faith actually looks like, rather than simply talk in theoretical terms" (p. 65). He then asks, "What are the fruits we should see in our lives that demonstrate a saving faith?"

Inserra gives seven evidences that one is truly born again: 1) manifesting "a life of repentance" (p. 66); 2) being "eternally minded" (p. 67); 3) believing "sound doctrine" (pp. 67-68); 4) practicing the "spiritual disciplines" (p. 68); 5) demonstrating "generosity" (p. 69); 6) having a "heart for those who don't know Christ" (pp., 69-70); and 7) having "love for God and His church" (p. 70).

If those are the evidences that one is born again, then no one can be sure that he is born again until he dies. Of course, anyone who holds to a strong view of the perseverance of the saints cannot be sure since even if one was highly confident he met those seven standards *now*, he could not be sure that he would continue to do so *until death*. Remember you need "a life of repentance," not a decade or two of repentance. You need all these seven criteria to be true of you until you die. If you fell away one day before you died, you would not find yourself with the Lord when you died.

The author gives his own testimony, indicating he was born again at a Fellowship of Christian Athletes retreat, simply by "a belief in the gospel of Christ," apart from any works on his part (p. 23). It sounds like he may well have believed in Christ for everlasting life and only later come under the teaching of Calvinism. Sadly, however, instead of proclaiming the message that he believed to be born again, he is proclaiming the message of Calvinism that he later learned.

I find it amazing that an author and a major publisher would put out a book that promotes the possibility of certainty that one is eternally secure when in fact that book teaches that certainty is impossible. I would think that anyone reading this book would feel that he was deceived. The actual title of this book should be: *Keeping Doubts Manageable: How to Have a High Level of Confidence That You Have the Marks of a True Christian.*

I recommend that anyone lacking assurance ask God for it and then read John's Gospel. That book will give assurance of everlasting life to anyone who is prayerful and open (e.g., John 3:14-18; 5:24; 6:35, 37, 39, 47; 11:25-27). (Both Shawn Lazar and I have books on assurance available at faithalone.org. However, while they are helpful, all that is needed to gain assurance is persistent prayer and God's Word, especially John's Gospel.)

I do not recommend Inserra's book *Without a Doubt.*

Robert N. Wilkin
Associate Editor
Journal of the Grace Evangelical Society

Grace Revolution: Experience the Power to Live Above Defeat. By Joseph Prince. New York, NY: FaithWords, 2015. 384 pp. Paper, $15.99.

In *Grace Revolution,* Joseph Prince notes that many people try to mix grace and law in Christian living: "Yet today many believers are still living in confusion, and get law and grace all mixed up by holding on to some aspects of the law and some aspects of grace in their Christian walk" (p. 9). Instead, Prince argues for what he considers a consistent grace position for Christian living. Grace is the only possibility for living a victorious Christian life: "The only way to help precious people overcome the power of sin is to preach them into God's amazing grace" (p. 25). Hence, this book is about sanctification in light of God's grace.

The book has several strengths and several weaknesses. Let me begin with the strengths.

Prince makes an excellent case that right living depends on right believing—echoing Scripture's teaching that we are transformed by renewing our minds (Rom 12:1-2). What we believe matters.

JOTGES readers will also strongly agree with Prince that not only is grace not a license to sin, but it alone "produces true holiness" (p. 60). Prince reports, "the more I preach God's amazing grace and unconditional love, the more my ministry office receives testimony after testimony from people who have been set free from all kinds of sins and addictions" (p. 26). And in support of that claim, the book reprints many of those encouraging testimonies.

Additionally, readers will also appreciate Prince's emphasis on knowing our position in Christ, and renewing our minds in light of that position. "When God's people are not established in their righteous identity in Christ, they become susceptible to the weapons of the enemy" (p. 106).

Lastly, Prince denunciations of both works salvation and legalistic forms of sanctification are much appreciated.

However, the book also has some weaknesses.

First, while Prince does quote Scripture, sometimes his interpretations are fanciful. For example, when he assigns meaning to each letter in the Hebrew word for *repentance* (e.g., "hei is the fifth letter in the Hebrew alphabet, and the number five in Bible numerics represents grace," p. 23) to eventually come up with the sentence: "Because of the cross, return to grace" (p. 23). That is not responsible Biblical interpretation, and not how you determine the meaning of a word.

Second, Prince is weak on God's discipline. He does affirm that believers can be disciplined, but not with "tragic accidents, sicknesses, and diseases" (p. 216). (What about the Corinthians?) That leads him to wrong interpretations of key passages such as the warning in Heb 10:26. Prince denies that warning applies to believers, in part, because he cannot imagine a believer going back to the sacrifices (p. 75). However, all the warnings in Hebrews are to believers. And is it so hard to imagine why a new Jewish convert facing social pressure from friends and family and outright political persecution might be tempted to return to Judaism? The question is, what is the consequence for that apostasy? Prince thinks that John 5:24 teaches that believers will not come into any judgment *at all* ("What is it that God wants us to be assured of? That we believers will never come into *krisis* judgment!" [p. 77]). Hence, Prince reasons that the judgment of Heb 10:27 cannot apply to believers. The answer to Prince's objection is to distinguish between types of judgment. While it is true that believers will not be judged *for their eternal salvation* (as per John 5:24), that does not mean they cannot experience God's *temporal judgment* for the sins they commit. God disciplines those He loves (Heb 12:6; Rev 3:19), and Paul relates that discipline to temporal "*krisis*" judgment (1 Cor 11:32). That explains why the Hebrews could experience God's judgment if they apostatized. All believers can experience that judgment for their sins (cf. Jas 5:12).

Third, Prince strongly rejects the distinction between legal forgiveness and parental forgiveness (pp. 285-90). He says that believers are totally forgiven. He used to think that 1 John 1:9 applied to believers, but that led him into a legalistic and obsessive approach to the confession of sins which nearly led to a breakdown: "The oppression grew so heavy that I felt my mind was about to snap!" (p. 79). Now he believes 1 John was not written to believers but to Gnostics who claimed that they had no sin (1:8, 10). According to Prince, John only begins to address believers ("my little children") in chap. 2. *JOTGES* readers will likely interpret all of 1 John as being about fellowship with God, which includes the ongoing fellowship forgiveness of 1 John 1:7, 9.

Fourth, Prince is unclear on the condition of salvation. Though he says, "There is no ambivalence in Scripture as to how a person becomes a born-again believer in Christ," I found that Prince was ambivalent. *JOTGES* readers know the one and only condition to be born again is *to believe* in Jesus for everlasting life (John 3:15-18, 36; 5:24; 6:47; Gal 2:16, etc.). To his credit, Prince often says we are saved "by grace through faith" (p. 55), which is very good. However, at other times he makes salvation depend upon inviting Jesus into your heart (p. 50), making a personal decision to receive the forgiveness of all their sins (pp. 52-53), confessing that Jesus is the resurrected Lord (p. 53), or by acknowledging and confessing your sinful state (p. 82). I think Prince really does believe in faith-alone salvation, but is inconsistent in his language, often using popular Christian phrases that actually confuse the issue of the one condition of salvation. It would be better if Prince was consistent in his faith message. It would also help if he reconsidered the role "confession" plays in the Christian life, especially in Romans (see Zane Hodges' *Romans: Deliverance from Wrath*).

Other strengths and weaknesses could be mentioned, but these will suffice. I hope that Prince's emphasis on grace gets a bigger hearing in the Charismatic world. I recommend this book for discerning readers.

Shawn Lazar
Associate Editor
Journal of the Grace Evangelical Society

We Will Not Be Silenced. **By Erwin W. Lutzer. Eugene, Oregon: Harvest House Publishers, 2020. 280 pp. Paper, $14.43.**

Erwin W. Lutzer served as senior pastor of Moody Bible Church for 36 years. He is a featured speaker on radio and has written several books. This is his most recent. There is a spiritual, cultural, and political war happening in America. So, the book is a call to arms! It is a call to understand the war that is being waged against the church in America. The enemy is trying to silence and then destroy the church and Biblical Christianity.

There are ten chapters in this book of 280 pages. It is engaging and easy to read. It is also well documented. Each chapter discusses an important issue about modern society. He begins with a summary describing the fundamental tools being used by the enemy. He identifies the enemy as those seeking to tear down and remake both America and the church. The strategies and tactics used by the enemy all come from communism.

Each chapter takes on a different issue confronting the church. The chapter on re-writing history shows how the enemy wants to delegitimize and erase our nation's Judeo-Christian heritage to make way for a godless secular society. This warning is reminiscent of Moses' warning to Israel in Deut 8:11-20.

The chapter on diversity shows how this strategy is being used to divide people and destroy civility. It is an attack on the unity of the church. Lutzer traces and documents the communist origins of this strategy.

The next chapter is about the attack on freedom of speech. While freedom of speech is a fundamental right guaranteed by the Constitution, the enemy wants to abolish it. There are those who want to silence Christians and the church. They want to stifle, silence, and shame anyone who believes what the Bible teaches.

Lutzer then shows how propaganda is used to wage the war of words. Satan is the father of lies so this should not come as a surprise. Propaganda is being used to deceive people and numb their thinking so they will not change their minds even when confronted by compelling evidence. It is the seed of delusion.

There is a chapter about sexualizing children. Lutzer documents the corrupting influence and role the public schools play in this. If the enemy can get children to think and engage in sexual activity early, then the corrupting effects of such activity will lead to more corruption and more confusion. Satan's desire is about getting the church and society to accept as normal the LGBTQ agenda. Even worse, this godless worldview is being shoved down the church's throat. To have a Biblical view of sexuality is to be a bigot, homophobe, hater, etc. What gets lost is that biology doesn't lie and neither does God!

Lutzer observes that the enemy sees capitalism as the disease and socialism/communism as the cure. This discussion is very relevant to the Free Grace movement. The doctrine of rewards is based on capitalism, whereby a person is rewarded for his/her work and effort. This is antithetical to socialism/communism.

One chapter discusses how radical Islam has joined forces with left-wing radicals in an attempt to destroy America and the church. Lutzer points out that both groups hate the Constitution and Christianity and are allied to bring them down. The discussion is interesting since these are strange allies. However, it shows how a common enemy can unite strange bed fellows for a season.

The final tool of the enemy is to vilify all opposition. No wonder we see so much shouting down in the public square. The author documents how this strategy comes directly from the proponents of communism. It explains why Christians and those who hold and declare Biblical values are called bigots, racists, haters, etc.

While the book is not about the content of the gospel, it may be relevant to sharing and declaring it. He says the gospel is the answer to these problems because they all originate with sinful mankind. True! So, Lutzer challenges Christians to understand people who have a worldview that is both antithetical to and hostile to God and the Bible.

GES readers may agree or disagree with Lutzer's proposed answers to the attacks being waged against Christians. But his diagnosis of the enemy's strategy and tactics is extremely accurate.

There are many endorsements of this book listed on the covers and inside. I agree with Dr. David Jeremiah, who said, "If I could, I would put this book into the hands of every Christian in America." I highly recommend this book.

Brad Doskocil
Chairman of the Board
Grace Evangelical Society

The Potter's Promise: A Biblical Defense of Traditional Soteriology. **By Leighton Flowers. NP: Trinity Academic Press, 2017. 175 pp. Paper, $16.91.**

Leighton Flowers is a former Calvinist Baptist minister and is currently the Director of Apologetics for Texas Baptists. In *The Potter's Promise,* he describes how he gave up on his belief in Calvinism. It took him three years of study to change his view.

The start of the journey occurred when he discovered that some writers he respected, like A. W. Tozer and C. S. Lewis, rejected the five points of Calvinism (p. 4). He came to reject the idea that God would create people for the "sole purpose of pouring out His everlasting wrath" on them in order to manifest His glory (p. 6). Flowers discovered that Romans 9 did not teach election of people to the lake of fire. After that, all his arguments in favor of Calvinism fell away. He adopted what he calls a "traditional" soteriology. Predestination means that God has predetermined that those who freely believe will be eternally saved. All believers have a responsibility to "humble themselves and trust Christ in faith."

In chap. 1, Flowers argues that the character of God argues against Calvinism. God is love. He loves His enemies. How could such a One create His enemies with no chance of being saved from an eternal hell? Romans 9 speaks of God choosing Jacob over Esau in order to be the one to carry God's blessing (p. 25).

Chapter 2 takes up that idea. The NT does speak of God choosing, but these elections are never for people to go to heaven or hell. God chose the nation of Israel through whom would come the Law, and they were to give it to the world. When it comes to salvation from hell, election is not unconditional. It refers to those who respond freely to God's invitation (p. 32).

God's sovereignty is a major emphasis of chap. 3. Flowers says it is not to be understood in the idea of God's determining everything that will happen, but in accomplishing His purposes in the free choices of every person. He also says that if Calvinism is true, God must have created evil. This was the position of Calvin himself (p. 43).

Chapter 4 has an interesting discussion on what it means when God hardens a person's heart. Flowers says that the Jews were self-hardened. They refused to believe and so God also hardened them in order to bring eternal salvation to the Gentiles (Romans 11, p. 48). The judicial hardening of God is directed towards those who are already rebellious and is always to accomplish a greater redemptive purpose. While it is great that Flowers rejects the Calvinistic view that God chooses people for hell or the kingdom, he assumes that the result of the hardening of the heart is in reference to eternal salvation. He does not consider that this hardening is describing a communal aspect that deals with other issues.

Flowers correctly points out that Christ elected the Twelve to be apostles and take the gospel to the world. He did not elect them to eternal life (p. 75). In addition, God elected Israel as a community (p. 80). Flowers says that the election in Ephesians 1 refers to the sanctification and glorification that all who believe in Jesus will receive because they have believed. He implies that progressive sanctification is guaranteed for every believer (pp. 78-79). Flowers also sees the universal aspect of God's election of the church in Ephesians 1 as well (p. 81). He rightly states that God elects nations and individuals to fulfill a purpose (p. 106).

When it comes to the foreknowledge of God, Flowers takes the position that this refers to believers in the OT whom God loved in the past. These believers will be conformed to the image of Christ because of His sacrifice on their behalf (pp. 90-91).

The biggest disappointment of this book is that Flowers does not clearly define what he means by "traditional soteriology." He rejects the Calvinistic doctrine, but it is difficult to determine what he believes is required of the unbeliever. Sometimes he only mentions the need for faith (pp. 47, 65, 81). In other places he says faith and repentance are necessary (pp. 64, 76, 105, 163), and in this regard the prodigal son's repentance is a picture of receiving eternal salvation. He sometimes says that the unbeliever needs to admit his sinfulness (p. 65) and implies that one needs to humbly ask for salvation.

Flowers does not appear to believe in rewards, so it is not surprising that he takes the position that passages that deal with rewards are speaking of eternal salvation (p. 88). Since he appears to believe in the perseverance of the saints in good works, he does not address the issue of assurance in this life.

Even though Flowers does not present a Free Grace gospel of eternal life and assurance, there is value in this book. It shows how a man steeped in a tradition can change his position. He correctly points out how Calvinists have misinterpreted passages about election and predestination. Many readers of the *JOTGES* will agree with many of his conclusions on these passages. Since Flowers once belonged to their camp, some Calvinists might be persuaded by his arguments in these areas more readily than they would from a proponent of Free Grace. For these reasons, I recommend the book.

Kathryn Wright
Missionary
Columbia, SC

Heaven and Hell: A History of the Afterlife. By Bart D. Ehrman. New York, NY: Simon & Schuster, 2020. 326 pp. Hardcover, $28.00.

What can an agnostic historian with atheist leanings tell us about heaven and hell? To those of us who believe the Bible, not much. Yet, he can tell us two important things. He can point out what people and religions have said about heaven and hell throughout history. In addition, he can demonstrate how to explain away certain parts of the Bible that mention these subjects.

Bart Ehrman is the James A. Gray Distinguished Professor of Religious Studies at the University of North Carolina, Chapel Hill. He is a leading secular authority on the NT and the history of early Christianity and has written or edited more than thirty books, some of which were *New York Times* bestsellers. He has also appeared on numerous television and radio programs and has been featured in leading newspapers and magazines.

Ehrman once claimed to be a "born-again Christian" who was "going to heaven" (p. xv), attended Moody Bible Institute, and finished his undergraduate degree at Wheaton College. After earning his PhD at Princeton Theological Seminary, he gradually "moved into a liberal form of Christianity" and finally "left the faith altogether" (p. xviii). Thus, it is no surprise that Ehrman believes that "the long book of Isaiah as it has come down to us is actually a combination of writings by different authors from different periods of history" (p. 97). He claims that the Book of Daniel was written "some four centuries later" than it claims to have been (p. 118), and that "some sayings attributed to Jesus are almost certainly things he did not say" (p. 148). Ehrman also believes that the Apostle Paul only wrote seven of the letters attributed to him (p. 170), that the Book of Acts "presents problems to historians" (p.170), and that the Book of Revelation is "full of symbols and is clearly meant to be interpreted figuratively" (p. 223).

In this book, Ehrman postulates that "the *ideas* of heaven and hell were invented and have been altered over the years" (p. xix). He maintains that the widely held view that there is a literal heaven and a literal hell "do not go back to the earliest stages of Christianity," "cannot be found in the Old Testament," and "are not what Jesus himself taught" (p. xix). Even within the NT and the writings of early Christians there are contradictions:

> The apostle Paul had different views of the afterlife from Jesus, whose views were not the same as those found in the Gospel of Luke or the Gospel of John or the book of Revelation. Moreover, none of these views coincides

exactly with those of Christian leaders of the second, third, and fourth centuries whose ideas became the basis for the understandings of many Christians today (p. xix).

Ehrman is not urging anyone "to believe or disbelieve in the existence of heaven and hell" (p. xx). Rather, he is interested in "seeing where these ideas came from within the dominant culture of the West, Christianity, especially as it emerged out of the pagan religions of its world and out of Judaism in particular" (p. xx). A fuller understanding of where these ideas came from can provide "assurance and comfort" because "even if we do have something to hope for after we have passed from the realm of temporary consciousness, we have absolutely nothing to fear" (p. xxiii).

Heaven and Hell can be loosely divided into two parts: the ideas of heaven and hell outside of the Bible (chaps. 1–4, 7, 12–14) and in the Bible (chaps. 5, 6, 8–11). The first chapter presents some fanciful guided tours of heaven and hell as found in early Christian writings. The next three chapters concern the ideas of heaven and hell in the ancient world. Chapters 5 and 6 focus on the afterlife in the OT. Chapter 7 deals with these topics in the apocryphal books of *1 and 2 Maccabees, 4 Ezra,* and *The Testament of Abraham.* Chapters 8–11 deal with what is said about these things in the NT. The last three chapters concern the resurrection of the body, ecstasy and torment in the afterlife, as well as purgatory, reincarnation, and universalism in early Christian writings. The book concludes with an afterword, notes, and an index.

In his chapters on the afterlife in the OT, Ehrman is actually not far off. He is certainly correct in saying that in "none" of the passages of the Hebrew Bible "can we find the traditional Christian views of the afterlife" (p. 92) and that "nowhere in the entire Hebrew Bible is there any discussion at all of heaven and hell as places of rewards and punishments for those who have died" (p. 83). However, the well-known passage in Job 19:25-27 about a future bodily resurrection ("For I know that my redeemer liveth …") is dismissed in a footnote: "Scholars have long recognized the massive problems attendant to these verses. The Hebrew text was jumbled over the course of its transmission, so that it is impossible to know how to translate the text or determine exactly what it means" (p. 391). Regarding the many that sleep in the dust of the earth that will awake "to shame and everlasting contempt" (Dan. 12:2), Ehrman says that it may well be that "they will be raised, shown the error of their ways, be put to shame, and then annihilated" (p. 123).

Ehrman divides the views of Jesus on the afterlife into two parts: the actual views of Jesus and the views attributed to Him. Ehrman believes that the four Gospels "can sometimes be highly problematic as guides to the actual words of Jesus" (p. 150). In fact, "Christian authors who later recorded Jesus's teachings actually altered his words in places to make them reflect their own understandings, which had developed over time after his death" (p. 191). This allows Ehrman to say that "Jesus did not teach that when a person died they would go to heaven or hell" (p. 154). He had "no idea of torment for sinners after death" (p. 155). The account of the rich man and Lazarus is just a parable, "not a literal description of reality" (p. 199). But regardless, "The historical Jesus himself did not tell the story of Lazarus and the rich man" (p. 202). Yet, "The doctrines of heaven and hell are rooted in this imaginative story attributed to Jesus only in Luke, a story that readers later took literally to describe what the afterlife would be like for the righteous and wicked" (p. 203). In his chapters on Paul and Revelation, Ehrman concludes that, like Jesus, they teach that the wicked will ultimately be annihilated.

In the end, Ehrman says that neither he nor anyone else has any way of knowing if "there is some other kind of afterlife existence" (p. 294). Although "the notion of a happy afterlife" is not as irrational as belief in "the fires of hell," Ehrman is "completely open to the idea and deep down hopeful about it." He admits that he really doesn't "believe it either" (p. 294). His sense is that "this life is all there is" (p. 294), and that in death we won't have consciousness because "we won't exist" (p. 295).

In the hands of the typical non-Christian or nominal American Christian, this is a dangerous book. Its message is, in general, that the Bible is contradictory, unreliable, and not what it claims to be. Specifically, it maintains that there is no judgment after death to be concerned about and certainly no such thing as hell. Even if there is, since "both Jesus and Paul believed that the wicked would be extermi-nated, never to live again" (p. 227), there is nothing to worry about. I can only think of two reasons to cautiously recommend this book to pastors. First, because Ehrman is such a good and popular writer, they should be familiar with his works and his arguments. Second, it is good to occasionally have our beliefs and traditions challenged.

Because a born-again Christian can't be unborn, I firmly believe that we will meet Bart Ehrman in heaven. Calvinists would say that because he did not persevere in the faith, this means that he was never saved in the first place. Arminians would say that he lost his salvation when he rejected Christianity. Others would say that he won't make it through the final judgment because he left the faith. Free Grace believers know better, even if Ehrman doesn't.

Laurence M. Vance
Vance Publications
Orlando, FL

Five Points Towards a Deeper Experience of God's Grace. By John Piper. Glasgow: Christian Focus Publications Ltd., 2017. 96 pp. Paper, $9.99.

John Piper is a popular writer and retired pastor. He is a devoted proponent of Reformed Theology and Calvinism. In this short book, Piper tries to answer the question, "How did God save me?" However, the real purpose of the book is to convince the reader that Calvinism is the only way people are saved.

Piper's answer to the question is the five points of Calvinism which are described by the acrostic TULIP. Each letter stands for one of the five points. He takes the standard Calvinistic view of each of the five points. Total depravity means complete inability to respond to God. Unconditional election means God picks the winners. Limited atonement is God's providing atonement through Christ's death for those who were lucky enough to be picked. Irresistible grace means the one who is picked cannot resist believing in Christ. He will believe. Perseverance of the saints means that all who believe will persevere to the end of their lives in faith. There is nothing new here in Piper's discussion

In presenting TULIP, Piper does one interesting thing. He rearranges the TULIP. He presents irresistible grace immediately after total depravity. He does this to establish the idea that God must regenerate a person before he ever believes in Jesus. In Piper's view, belief is a gift, and thus a person must be regenerated before actually believing in Jesus. The Bible does not teach this; rather we become a child of God when we believe (e.g., John 3:16; 6:35; Gal 3:26). Belief comes first!

Included throughout the book are references to the sovereignty of God. In Calvinism, the sovereignty of God is a prominent theme. In fact, Calvinists overemphasize it to the detriment of God's other attributes. Piper is no exception.

Piper attempts to refute criticisms of Calvinism throughout his discussion and does so in subtle and potentially convincing ways. However, one who is well grounded in what the Bible says will see through these attempts.

Piper writes very well. His work can be quite convincing to those not familiar with Calvinism. I do not recommend this book, except for well-grounded pastors who want to gain a better understanding of this false theology and how Calvinists like Piper twist the Scriptures to fit their theology.

Brad Doskocil
Chairman of the Board
Grace Evangelical Society

An Unconventional God: The Spirit According to Jesus. By Jack Levison. Grand Rapids, MI: Baker Academic, 2020. 226 pp. Paper, $21.38.

Levison is the W. J. A. Power Professor of Old Testament Interpretation at the Perkins School of Theology, Southern Methodist University in Dallas, TX. This book deals with the role of the Holy Spirit in the life of Jesus. As an OT scholar, Levison seeks to show that this role is predicted in the OT and that through the power of the Spirit, Jesus fulfilled these predictions. While Levison does not believe in the verbal inspiration of the Scriptures, he does want to determine what the original writers say about the subject. The writers believed that God wanted to reveal Himself and does so through the Spirit working through the Son (p. 89). At the same time, Levison admits that the Jesus of history is different from the Jesus interpreted in each Gospel (p. 205).

According to Levison, without the Jewish Scriptures we cannot understand how the writers understood the Holy Spirit (p. 193). An example of this is found in the Lord's teaching on the blasphemy against the Holy Spirit. Levison says that the meaning is found in the discussion of the Exodus as described in Isaiah 63. Israel rebelled against the guiding angel, and Jesus warns His listeners not to do the same against the Spirit (p. 195). Levison does not discuss what the results of this blasphemy would be or if believers can commit this sin. He does not see the sin as a danger only in the first century.

Levison makes the observation that in the life of the Lord, the Spirit often brought suffering and difficulties. This work eventually led to His death. The work of the Spirit in the life of believers will often result in persecution and trouble (p. 122).

This reviewer appreciated the author's discussion of John 3 and the Lord's interaction with Nicodemus. He correctly points out that Jesus uses a play on words. The Greek word describing the new birth can either be "from above" or "again," and Nicodemus misunderstands the Lord (pp. 137-38). The word "spirit" can also be understood as wind. Levison correctly points out that Jesus is telling Nicodemus he needs a new birth from above by the Holy Spirit.

Levison also correctly notes that when Jesus says we must be born of water and spirit/wind, He is speaking of two things in close association with each other since only one preposition governs both nouns. This "symbiosis" existed in the religious climate of first-century Judaism. The Qumran community, for example, taught that its members must be cleansed by water and Spirit (p. 140). The recognition that the two words are connected is helpful, but it is better to see both water and wind as referring to the Holy Spirit. Levison does not discuss this possibility from the OT.

Like the vast majority of Evangelical scholars, Levison sees the Gospel of John as a book that emphasizes dualities. These include: birth from above versus birth from below; truth versus falsehood; light versus darkness; and Spirit versus flesh (p. 203). Unfortunately, he sees the Gospel of John as being written by a community of Christians in the second century. The discussion of cleansing by water, in his opinion, reflects the "mystery" of baptism in the early church, where the Spirit is at work in the water. When one emerges from the water of baptism, the Spirit also gives new birth (p. 141).

When the Spirit is mentioned in the Gospels, Levison sees many allusions in the OT. Readers of the *JOTGES* will probably conclude that some of these allusions have merit, while others do not. He maintains that the birth of Jesus through the Spirit reminds the reader of the creation of the world when the Spirit hovered over the face of the deep (Gen 1:1-2; p. 13). The announcement to Mary that the Spirit will overshadow her finds an OT reference in how the Spirit of God overshadowed the tabernacle in the wilderness (p. 21). Also in the birth narratives, the prophet Simeon is well versed in the teachings of the Spirit from the Book of Isaiah (pp. 7, 130). As many have noted, as does Levison, the prophet Isaiah's writings about the Spirit are found in the accounts of Jesus' baptism and in His first sermon in Nazareth (pp. 58-61, 198).

Readers will probably agree with Levison that Jesus' being driven by the Spirit into the wilderness has parallels in some way with the Exodus generation (pp. 180-81). In addition, the dove sent out by Noah after the Flood may be the OT background to the Spirit as a dove at the baptism of the Lord. In both cases, the dove hovers over water (p. 53). However, Levison's view that the Lord's giving of the Spirit, instead of snakes and scorpions, to those who ask Him finds its source in the wilderness of the Exodus will leave many readers scratching their heads (pp. 92, 196).

This book is a mixed bag. It does not exegete Biblical passages. The writer is not what the readers of the *JOTGES* would define as conservative. He is certainly not Free Grace. But he does desire to determine authorial intent in the teachings concerning the Spirit in the four Gospels. The strength of the book is in its discussions of possible OT backgrounds to the work of the Spirit in these books. Each reader will conclude that some are valid, while others are not. I recommend the book for those discussions that possibly do have validity.

Kenneth W. Yates
Editor
Journal of the Grace Evangelical Society

Made in the USA
Columbia, SC
23 November 2021

49647054R00059